MODERN PRINCIPLES ANALYSIS OF RESOURCE FLOWS IN CRISIS CONDITIONS
CULTURE AND CREATIVE INDUSTRY

ANDREY P. GARNOV
NATALIA A. MALSHINA

Translator: Daria V. Dementieva, Russia

ACADEMUS
Publishing

Academus Publishing
2020

ACADEMUS
Publishing

Academus Publishing, Inc.

1999 S, Bascom Avenue, Suite 700 Campbell CA 95008
Website: www.academuspublishing.com
E-mail: info@academuspub.com

The research is implemented within the grant of the Russian Foundation for Basic Research No. 19-010-01004\20 "Development of Organizational, Economic and Financial Mechanisms of Support and Strategic Development of the Cultural Industry in the Regions of Russia"

The right of Andrey P. Garnov, Doctor of Economics, Professor, Head of the Department of Economics and Production Organization of Plekhanov Russian University of Economics, Honorary Worker of Higher Professional Education of the Russian Federation (2012), Honored Worker of Buryatia (2007), Chairman of the UMS UMO on the Profile "Economics of Enterprises and Organizations", Moscow, Russia;

Nataliya A. Malshina, Doctor of Philosophy, Associate Professor of the Department of Humanities of the Saratov State Conservatory named after L.V. Sobinov, Master of Economics (Moscow), Moscow, Russia.

Translator: Daria V. Dementieva, Moscow, Russia.

For e-mail correspondence:
Garnov A.P. — profgarnov@yandex.ru
ORCID: https://orcid.org/0000-0003-1435-8698, SPIN-code: 8960-6025, Author ID: 295432

Malshina N.A. — sgk@freeline.ru
ORCID: https://orcid.org/0000-0003-1632-538X, Researcher ID: P-5750-2019

Dementyeva D.V. — dasha160370@icloud.com, npp-f@yandex.ru;
ORCID: https://orcid.org/0000-0001-9123-9866, Researcher ID: Y-7312-2018

ISBN 10: 1 4946 0018 8
ISBN 13: 978 1 4946 0018 1
DOI 10.31519/978-1-4946-0018-1

The culture industry should become attractive for capital investment through the development of organizational-economic mechanisms of support in the form of integrated structures as well as through the development of mechanisms of its financing: systems of culture multi-channel backing and state-private partnership which would allow to create prerequisites for the appearance and implementation of new ideas and projects in the culture field, contributing to culture sphere formation as a full-fledged source of state income.

As a result of this project implementation, original new fundamental theoretical assumptions and empirical data in the culture industry field and the regional development have been obtained.

The project focuses on the study of fundamental basics research of the culture industry functioning, solves scientific problems of the culture industry effectiveness evaluation and direction justification of its support and funding; there are being worked out strategies and mechanisms of the culture industry efficiency development and increase in accordance with the characteristics and needs of regional economies.

CONTENTS

ABBREVIATIONS

BCG	—	Boston Consulting Group
CI	—	Culture Institution
CLI	—	Culture Logistic Institution
DEA	—	Data Development Analysis
DVR	—	Department of Visas and Registration
EU	—	European Union
EEU	—	European Economic Union
EAEU	—	Euro Asian Economic Union
IT	—	Information Technology
ICT	—	Information Communication Technologies
GDP	—	Gross Domestic Product
LAN	—	Local Area Nerwork
LC	—	Logistic Center
LCC	—	Life Cycle Contracts
LFF	—	Logistic Financial Flow
PPP	—	Public Private Partnership
RF	—	Russian Federation
SWOT	—	Strengths, Weaknesses, Opportunities, Threats (analysis)
UNCTAD	—	United Nations Conference on Trade and Devrelopment
VR	—	Virtual Reality
WTO	—	World Trade Organization

INTRODUCTION

Strategic development and tactical improvement of culture and creativity industry can bring up to 30% of state income with great probability (an attraction of foreign tourists, students, a mobility of consumers of culture, tourism services, etc.).

Certain vacuum occurs in the matters of relationships between state, business and culture. The culture industry should become attractive for capital investment through the development of project activities, organizational-economic mechanisms of support in the form of integrated structures as well as through the development of mechanisms of its financing: systems of culture multi-channel backing and state-private partnership which would allow to create prerequisites for the appearance and implementation of new ideas and projects in the culture field, contributing to culture sphere formation as a full-fledged source of state income. Based on the research relevance, the tasks, solved in the project, are:

- Theory and methodology development of culture industry research within modern trends of digital economy development;
- Analysis and assessment of service market development degree and potential definition of culture industry development;
- Research hypothesis testing about presence and degree influence of culture industry functioning on Russia economic growth and methodology work-out for impact assessment of culture industry on economic growth;
- Development of organizational-economic mechanisms for culture industry development in the form of clusters and integrated service complexes in the RF regions;
- Financing processes research and the application of its new forms to culture industry;
- Development of concept of models for integrated service complexes in culture industry as a mechanism for the development and support of culture industries with service complexes founded upon various financing models;

As a result of this project implementation, original new fundamental theoretical assumptions and empirical data in the culture industry field and the regional development will be obtained.

The project focuses on the study of fundamental basics research of the culture industry functioning, solves scientific problems of the culture

5

industry effectiveness evaluation and direction justification of its support and funding; there are being worked out strategies and mechanisms of the culture industry efficiency development and increase in Russia regions in accordance with the characteristics and needs of regional economies.

It is stereotypically considered that the culture sphere is traditionally a subsidized branch of intangible sphere. Stereotypically, the culture industry is considered as one of the cost items and is on state budget financing but, according to developed countries statistics, it constitutes 5% of GDP and is a large and profitable sector. Basing on multiyear European and whole world experience development, one can testify to that the culture industry, the creative industry are mass consumers attraction centers. Consumer attracted fund flow has a rapid turnaround and, therefore, brings a tangible and rapid income. Global mechanism for financial flow management in the culture industry has not been applied and requires adaptation to Russian practice.

In the Russian Federation, there is a lack of effect managements onto the culture industry. The culture industry strategic development and its tactical improvement, with a very high probability, can bring up to 30% of state revenue (an attraction of foreign tourists, students, a mobility of culture services, tourism consumers etc.)

In Russian Federation, there are neither state or political structures and traditions which could successfully implant these new systems in. A certain vacuum occurs in the relationships between state, business and culture.

In the world economy, there are already proven and bringing a stable and increasing income mechanisms and the culture industry support organizational models in dependence to industry branch lifecycle stage of particular regional entity and its demands.

It is necessary to exploit financial, guarantee schemes and financial-credit mechanisms that are productional, market, educational, managerial and political ones — mechanisms of the culture industry support that are being developed in the current project.

Economy, organization and management in the culture industry represent a relatively new research direction and, above all, they have got theoretical and practical justification in foreign scientists' studies. From the middle of C20th and onward, in the modern society, a new social, economic and cultural significance of the culture industry has formed which has become the basis of "cultural production era " explored in the works of D. Hezmondalsh[1].

---

[1] Hezmondalsh D. Cultural Industries; *HSE* 2014, p. 81 *(in Russian)*.

Theoretical approaches to the concept of creative economy and the definition of creative industries, considering this sphere as an articulated connection of creative innovations and economic activity of subjects, institutionalization of the culture industry concept and its main elements (a creative class, a cluster, an artistic organization) are presented in the works of modern foreign researchers[1].

Business structures model of the cultural industries is explored in the works of Bourbieu P. and consists of "concentrated circles which center are the art-industries in, and all others form self- layers or circles, located around the center, extending more and more farther as the creative ideas usage is being included into a wider production context"[2].

In Throsby D.'s works, it is presented a centralized model of the cultural industries, it includes two main circles[3]. In the classic essay by V. Benjamin, the culture industry progressive potential is seen in the spread of mechanization and mass production to the culture field, he associates this process "with ever increasing masses significance in the modern life" distinguished by "tendency of the uniqueness overcoming of any givenness" and considers it as potentially progressive[4].

Also, in foreign literature, concepts of "cultural industry" and "mass culture" are differentiated[5]. Cultural artifacts are subdued now to the

---

[1] Hawkins J. Creative Economy. How to Turn Ideas into Money. 2011, p. 256; Newbigin J. Creative Economy. Mapping. *M: "Creative economy"* 2011 *(in Russian)*; Matthews M. Science and Innovation Policy and the New (and Old) Economics of Creativity. *Creative Destruction* 2008. Vol. 1, No. 1; Potts J., Cunningham St., Hartley J., Ormerod P. Social Network Markets: A New Definition of the Creative Industries. *Creative Destruction* 2008. Vol. 1, No. 1; Kate Morrison and Jason Potts.Industry Policy as Innovation Policy.*Creative Destruction* 2008. Vol. 1, No. 1; C. Mellander, R. Florida. Creative Class or Human Capital.*Creative Destruction* 2008.Vol. 1, No. 1; Richard Caves. Creative Industries: Contracts Between Art and Commerce. *Harvard University Press: Harvard* 2000; Fassel P. Creative Class. http://hiki.gorod.tomsk.ru/index-1253025448.php*(in Russian)*; Florida R. Creative Class. People Who Change the Future. 2005. 430 p. http://www.creativeclass.com/richard_florida; Hesin E. Great Britain: Economy Recessions and Revivals. *World Economy and International Relationships* 2000. No. 8 *(in Russian)*: Castels M. Formation of Society of Network Structures. New Post-industrial Wave in West.Anthology. *M.* 1999. 594 p. *(in Russian)*.
[2] Bourbieu P. The Field of Cultural Production: Essays on Art and Literature / R. Jonson. *Cambridge: Polity press* 1993, 21 p.
[3] Throsby D. Economy and Culture. *M. Ed. House. High School of Economic* 2013, p. 159 *(in Russian)*.
[4] Benjamin V. Piece of Art in Era of its Technical Reproducibility. *Moscow: Cultural Center Named after Goethe Medium* 1996. 240 pages, p. 196 *(in Russian)*
[5] Adorno T. W. Culture Industry Reconsidered, in Culture Industry / R. W. Witkin, Adorno on Popular Culture, p. 85; Bernstein J. M. Introduction to Adorno's Culture Industry. *London and New York.*2008. p. 13

logic profitability and capital accumulation with greater regularity. Critical potential of intellectual culture is undermined by the conformist or "affirmative" products of the cultural industry; the products facilitate individuum adaptation to capitalism; various techniques are used for this, there are of: "standardization", "pseudo-individualization" (introduction of minor plot differences, obscuring general formula), "reaction mechanisms" (voice-over laughter that guarantees "correct " audience reaction)[1].

---

[1] Held. Introduction to Critical Theory. T. W. Adorno. How to look at television. *Culture industry*, p. 94.

1. GLOBAL TRENDS IN MANAGEMENT OF CULTURESERVICESIN CRISIS CONDITIONS

In the world economy, provenmechanisms which bring stable and growing income, and structural models for support in the culture industry depending on the stage of the life cycleof a given organizational unit and its needs, already exist.

According to World Bank data the creative economy constitutes about 7% of World Gross Domestic Product (GDP). According to United Nations (UN) data the annual increase in growth of the creative economy is at least 8.7%.According to the European Commissionreport "The Economics of Culture in Europe", one effect of the culture industry is to provide growth of new jobs, the multiplier effect and the contribution to GDP of which constitutes 5.3%. The culture sector employs 3.4% of the population. The culture sphere is considered in Western countries as one of the important sectors of the economy and investment (Table 1).

Table 1. Projections, assistance and income Indices (1975 = 100)

Annee	Projections	Assistance	Recettes
2017	405,4431	97,0824	303,706
2016	409,4	92,8	289,6
2015	410,3	99,8	304,7
2014	400,1	93,8	285,5
2013	408,4	105,2	328,8
2012	401,2	105,2	322,7
2011	400,6	110,7	335,4
2010	408,9	119,1	350,1

Sources: Institut de la statistique du Québec (ISQ), Updated: August 22, 2018.

The growth rate of international trade in the cultural services was 3% in 2016 according to UNCTAD statistical data. A larger increase was observed only in the trade in computer and information services (4.5%). All this testifies to the growing importance ofthe contribution of the culture industry to economic development in modern conditions and to the prospects for the development of the culture industry.

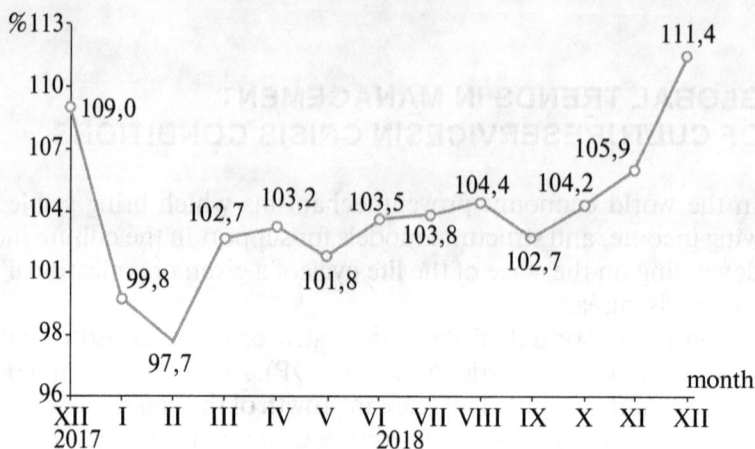

Figure 1.1. Volume dynamics of paid services to the population (prices expressed in terms of average monthly value of 2015) [5]

The total volume of trade goods in the culture and creativity (creative products) industries was 510 billion dollars . According to UNCTAD and WTO data, the greatest participant in the culture and creativity industry international market was China (169 billion dollars), followed by the USA (41 billion dollars) and France (34 billion dollars).

A gradual positive trend is observed in 2016, which strengthens towards the end of the year, however, at the beginning of 2017, it demonstrates the lowest indicators (Figure 1.1). The population was provided with paid services of 8377.8 billion rubles in 2016, in December 2016 with 764.0 billion rubles, and in 2017-8, there was a stable position in paid culture services to the population (Table 1.2).

Expenses expressed as specific weight of the payment of services in consumer expenditure constituted 21.4% in 2016 in comparison with 20.7% in 2015; in December 2016the figure was 19.5% in comparison with 18.8% in December 2015.

The UN report "Creative economy" provides data on Russia: services in the field of culture employed 7.3% of the population, the contribution of the culture sector to Russia's GDP is 6% (equivalent to a third of collected taxes on production and imports and is comparable to the contributions of such industries as the production and distribution of electricity, gas and water (3.9%), healthcare and social services (4.5%), public administration and military security (4.9%), agriculture, hunting and forestry (5.1%). A significant part of state subsidies directed into the area of culture isreturned to the state directly or indirectly.

10

Table 1.2. The structure of paid servicesinbillion of rubbles 2017—2018

	year	*1st quarter*	*1st half year*	*9 months full year*	*inpercentage to total*
Paid services to the population – in total	100	100	100	100	100
Percentages:					
telecommunications	14.4	14.3	14.1	14.2	14.1
culture	1.7	1.8	1.8	1.7	1.7
tourism	1.6	1.1	1.3	1.6	1.6
physical culture and sports	0.8	1.0	0.8	0.8	0.8
hotels and similar accommodations	2.5	2.1	2.5	2.8	2.6
including health resort organizations	1.4	0.9	1.1	1.4	1.3
education systems	6.7	7.1	6.7	6.5	6.8

There are some successfully implemented social and cultural business projectsto be found currently in the world. For example, Le Centquatre[1] — a cultural cluster on a democratic format in a huge industrial building of the early XX century, where everyone can find something to do. It hosts large exhibitions ofstars like Anthony Gormley and Keith Haring, concerts, various art festivals,it also puts on performances and theatrical productions.

Also, there is the project of the Louis Armstrong Museum extension by Caples Jefferson Architects[2]. The house museum of one of the world'sgreatest jazz musicians is located in the Corona district of Queens, New York, where immigrants have settled over time. In addition to exhibition tours, the Museum hosts lectures and jazz concerts which are very popular with the public who come here up from all over the world. The space of the former garage which was fitted for public events, could not cope with the influx of Armstrong admirers. The administration of the Museum decided in 2007 to expand the building and construct an educational center building. The office of Caples Jefferson Architects

---

[1] www.104.fr.
[2] http://art-and-houses.ru/2017/08/02/proekt-rasshireniya-muzeya-lui-armstronga-ot-caples-jeffersonarchitects/.

ofNew York was commissioned to design the project. The project, which cost $23 million, was approved by the City Council. A building of just under 14,000 square feet will be built across the street from the Museum and is scheduled to open in 2019. According to the project, on the first floor, spaces are provided for a jazz club of 68 seats, an exhibition gallery, and a museum shop. The Director wants to place archives and offices on the second floor of the educational center.

The first successfully implemented social-cultural business projects appeared also in Russia in the form of the TEXTIL cultural center, Yaroslavl[1]. In 2013, the art critic YuliaKrivtsova and architect Sergey Kremnev proposed to the factory "KrasnyPerekop" administration to open the TEXTIL cultural center on the site of the former cotton warehouse. The center hosts large joint dinners, lectures, markets, children's festivals and city weekends. For several years, an active group has formed around the project: working meetings are held weekly where anyone who is willing can attend. It is at these meetings where decisions on how the space will develop further will be made.

The art space platform "The Gates" in the city of Kaliningrad appeared in 2013 in a historic building at Zachhaim Gates. It was launched by a group of independent trustees and former Chairman of Photographers' Union of Kaliningrad, Yuri Seliverstov. Small exhibitions, bric-a-brac markets and other events started at the "Gates". The room spaces were repaired, electricity was installed, windows were replaced and money was sought for the development together with volunteers. Over time a gallery of contemporary art for young people, a coffee shop "Bread and Turk" and a co-working "Table Chair" have been formed there. The art platform supports young artists, creates facilities for their selfexpression, and develops the creative industries of the city[2].

In the conditions of the intensified economic crisis, problems of optimization and saving of various types of resources are of particular relevance. The process of consumption and constant renewal of resources, ("cashflow") i.e. the continuity of resource flows, is the main mode of enterprise existence, as in any business activity. The structure of motion by a flow principle requires coordination of participants; one participant may not give the expected results due to inconsistency with the capabilities of other participants. Resource flows connect partners taking part in the structure of the motion, and require coordinated efforts to minimize losses which arise when flows cross the boundaries of logistics systems.

---

[1] http://textil.in/
[2] http://blog.vector.education/posts/kulturnie-tsentri-v-kotorih-hochetsya-pobivat.

The necessity and possibility of integration processes in the service market are also conditioned by the rapid development of computer information systems.

Coordination of effort and integration of resources are necessary within the limits of each individual enterprise; they are the logistics optimization basis of its activities. However, integration inside a company cannot have a significant impact on environmental factors. The maximum effect can be obtained by optimizing flows throughout their entire length from the first stage of production to consumption. All links of the logistics chain must work consistently as a single system. At the same time, the movement of all kinds resource flow, not just material ones, but also information, finance and services, should be coordinated. Thus following trends of integration exist:

- coordination of flows moving at all stages of progression to final consumer as a result of final buyers requirements;
- integration of economic flows of different kinds;
- integration of technologies used by participants of biblio-production moving process.

Success in integration processes is possible if the following requirements are met:

- informational openness of business partners;
- strict compliance with the requirements imposed by each subsequent link of the logistics chain upon the results of previous links;
- coordination of joint work planning;
- working out standards and other documents that unify the requirements for job results

In these ways, the goal of the logistics system and the composition of the necessary functions and work types to ensure goal achievement are determined initially. Then, on the basis of the most effective achievement of the logistics system goal, efforts are made to adjust separate kinds of expenditure to gain their gross sum reduction.

The approach is used in the logistics which has been named as an analysis of "bottlenecks" (critical resources). Any resource limitation takes place at any given time moment in the logistics system, otherwise, it would develop endlessly. First of all, a system development rate depends on the efficiency of critical (insufficient) resources usage. The usage efficiency upturn of other resources, called noncritical resources, hardly affects system development. Taking into account this regularity, it should be, for instance, aimed, in the periods of decrease of customer flows when the burden on bookstore salesmen is reduced (i.e. the personnel resource becomes non-critical one), to provide them the opportunity to use the labor time reserve for improving qualifications, cross professional training and so on. Critical resources (causing bottlenecks) constrain the development of the system. The viability of the logistics system primarily depends on the weakest system link.

On the basis of this principle, the law of link strength of the logistics chain has been formulated which states: the throughput capacity (productivity) of each consequent link of the logistics chain must be not less than the throughput capacity of the previous link:

$$P_i \leq P_i + 1,$$

where P_i is the throughput capacity of the logistics chain link; $i = 1,...,$ n is the quantity of logistics chain links.

If this law is violated, resources excessive reserves are formed hindering the economic flows moving along the channel.

The theory and practice of foreign companies proves the effectiveness of this approach in resource management. The use of the basic statements of the logistics approach as well as of individual logistics principles to improve the efficiency of economic resources management will allow the possibility of increasing the logistics systems stability of the service and tourism sector by the way of their closer interaction through integration both in the logistics chain itself and with the dynamic external environment. The integrated approach makes it possible to combine functional areas of the logistics by coordinating actions performed by independent parts of the logistics system, sharing common responsibility within the target function.

The modern concept of resource management leans on strategic management which is aimed, among other things, at the formation of an innovative culture in a company (we mean a stable set of certain type abilities). The culture of innovations comes into being as a result of the implementation of an innovation strategy of which the main elements are:
- focus on the customer (the creation of a system of continuous monitoring of customer satisfaction and the adaptation of a company to changes in customers' preferences, the analysis of the long-term development of needs and providing for an advanced development of the product or service);
- leadership of managers;
- employees involvement in the generation of innovation;
- implementation of continuous improvements (kaizen);
- application of a process approach for operational control [5].

14

All the prerequisites of the formation of an innovative culture of economic entities are created in supply chains today. It becomes possible to focus on the consumer due to tight integration, because the modern logistics concept of the creation of added value puts the consumer first. At the same time, the innovative mechanism of logistics tools enables the forecasting of consumer preferences development, science and technology development, and market opportunities [5]. The use of the logistics management tools in the service sector also shows innovation.

In the conditions of profound economic crisis, issues of the effective management of resource potential and, therefore the rational use of resources, come to the fore. The logistics mobilization of all managing reserves is of particular importance for the social-cultural services sphere at the present stage of market relations in Russia. The resource saving for the rapidly developing services sector of Russia will boost competitiveness in the world market.

REFERENCE LIST

1. Exploring the Northern Dimension, available at: http://www.ndin-stitute.org.
2. Garnov A.P., Kireeva N.S. Financial, Material and Informational Flows: Interaction Point in Logistics // RISK: Resources, Information, Supply, Competition. — 2017. — No. 2. pp. 48–51 *(in Russian)*.
3. Garnov A., Kireeva N. Strategic Planning and Management as Basis for Business Value Increasing by Multi-link Logistics Chains / / Logistics. — 2012. No. 1 (62). — pp. 20–23 *(in Russian)*.
4. Garnov A.P., Kireeva N.S. Logistics Tools. — Moscow: Creative Economics, 2009 *(in Russian)*.
5. Kireeva N.S. Innovative Mechanism of Management.

2. METHODOLOGICAL BASES OF DEVELOPMENT MECHANISM OF CULTURE AND CREATIVITY INDUSTRY

Since the 70s of C20th, structural changes and shifts have been taking place in economy which have radically transformed ratios of economy sectors. Trends of modern human society development — globalization, post-industrialization, trans-nationalization, softization, financialization, Informatization and innovatization — impact the economy and the society causing a quantitative and qualitative influence on relationship between their sectors, act as new and significant factors of economic development maintaining competitiveness of modern economy countries. The process of deindustrialization and economic growth, oriented mainly on the service sector development, has started to lead quicker than the industry in all the countries. As a result of these processes, the service sector is at the leading place in economically developed countries.

Further global integration of society, culture and business requires new mechanisms to ensure the culture industries development in the RF in the light of world development experience, resource potential usage maximization and verified organizational-economic management mechanisms adoption for the culture industry development.

At the moment, the underdevelopment of organizational-economic forms and the lack of mechanisms readiness for a support and a strategic development of the culture industry inhibits this sphere progress, and the structure of investment sources of socio-cultural projects of the RF reveals a disproportion between public and private sectors and an asymmetry between demands and opportunities of these projects financing.

The culture industry should become attractive for capital investment through project activities development, organizational-economic mechanisms support in the form of integrated structures, clusters and service complexes as well as through mechanisms development of its financing: multi-channel financing systems of the culture sphere and public-private partnership which would create preconditions for the emergence and implementation of new ideas and projects in the culture field, enabling its formation as a full source of state income. These aspects of the culture industry development problematics are insufficiently exploited that confirms their novelty and high relevance by.

The possibility of Russian society effective response to big challenges amid interaction between a man and a nature, a man and a technology, social institutions at the present step of global development also applying humanitarian and social sciences methods comes on the scene.

The questions of study and development of organizational-economic and financial mechanisms to support the culture industry are not widely presented in foreign and domestic works, the research in this direction is only beginning to develop and represents particular practical interest. Project expected results have no analogues *in Russian* science, they will complement existing methods of support of the culture industry and its funding sources development and can be presented as Russian science achievements in the field of the culture industry research *in Russian* conditions.

An essential element of scientific novelty of the current study is in its object — the culture industry and its characteristics research *in Russian* regions, considered by the authors of the project as an assemblage of the culture sphere public and private institutions functioning on the territory of a region (a federation subject), and an interconnection of subjects in interaction integration forms in regional economy.

The main research hypothesis of the project is composed on search of interconditionality and interdependence of region economic growth upon culture industry functioning efficiency why the strengthening of cooperation and cluster-linkages between its subjects creates conditions for regional economy revitalization and sustainable economic growth. To this end, the project analyzes the conditions and quantifies the effectiveness of the culture industry functioning in the modern circumstance. Based on these findings, the project develops a complex of organizational-economic and financial mechanisms on the culture industry development and support.

The novelty of the project set tasks is also in the development of theoretical-methodological messages and the creation of methodological recommendations on efficiency assessment of culture industry regional systems on the basis of DEA (Data EnvelopmentAnalysis) methodology and in working out of organizational-economic mechanisms of the culture industry development in RF regions in the form of clusters and integrated service systems, of financing mechanisms on the basis of public-private partnership mechanisms which are capable to heighten efficiency realization of big ambitious investment projects in the culture industry on the backs of private business participation therein, to provide for the sector progression and budget burden lowering, to attract the best management personnel and technologies, to enhance service quality of end customers, to concentrate attention of government bodies on the most appropriate for them administrative functions and to narrow down projects risks by means of their distribution between private partner and authorities.

Despite diversified approaches, methods and indicators reality, there is no currently accepted methodology, research tools and organizational-financial maintaining of the culture industry today *in Russian* practice. The research in this direction is just starting to proceed and to demonstrate considerable scientific and practical interest.

Culture institutions interrelation aspects with key subjects in region are not sufficiently studied, this brings to that culture industry progression issues at system-level remain unexplored. The novelty high degree of the obtained results is also due to that the current project is a pilot research. These methodological data have not been developed that confirms their novelty since the project results have no analogues *in Russian* science and practice.

Research methodological base consists of fundamental scientific works by domestic and foreign researchers on culture and art sphere functioning theory and practice, service activities specifics, culture industry financing mechanisms and specificities as well as on system analysis works, theoretical-methodological bases of integrative processes and relations, on evaluation problems of resources potential and their usage efficiency improvement.

During the research, general scientific cognition methods will be exploited: induction and deduction, abstracting, analysis, systematization, structuring, classification. Brought tasks solution is based on the application of methods of institutional, economic and statistical analysis, time-series analysis, comparative and system analysis, correlational-regressive analysis, organizational-economic modeling, expert assessments.

In particular, the presence of correlation and influence degree of culture industry development level on economic growth will be determined by means of correlational-regressive analysis that will allow to establish direct and inverse relations between variables by their absolute values and to assess accurately this relation tightness. To check the regression equitation, it is supposed to use Pearson's code, Fisher's ratio test and Student's t-test. Modified «knowledge production function» of Cobb-Douglas in A. Jaffe augmentation, Herfindahl-Hirschmann concentration ratio, Malkmist index for model building of the efficiency assessment of regional culture industries.

For uncovering of factors influence, determining the preferred subjects of integrated service complexes deploying, match factorial analysis method will be actualized by of either complex or system study and of factors impact measurement per successive index value getting quantitative and qualitive assessment.

While the results rating of the culture and art industry functioning and while the study of nonlinear processes of the culture and art industry influence on Russian Federation particular regional subject, correlational-regressive analysis method will be used.

Data intellectual analysis methods will allow to pursue the analysis of functioning effectiveness of the culture industry regional systems.

To create typologies and ranking of the culture industry by Russia regions, the classification, positioning, ranking and clusterization approaches will be exploited. To evaluate higher education sector efficiency by RF regions and efficiency ranking composition of regions by the culture industry boost level, the method of integral ranking analysis and of indicators multidimensional ranking will be applied.

For to get an objective picture while complex research pursuing on complex investigations on the evaluation of trends of the culture industry progression and efficiency, the standard data collection methods will be applied for, including formalized surveys, expert interviews and focus-groups, some indicators monitoring of the culture sphere development, statistics data analysis of Rosstat (Russian Federal State Statistics Service) and RF Ministry of Culture.

Evaluation of the effectiveness of regional systems is proposed to base on the methodology of DEA (Data Envelopment Analysis — data shell analysis or functioning environment analysis) which allows to compare the activity of complex economic systems on the ground of the analysis of non-discrete parameters of these systems functioning by reference to the statement, that culture industry regional systems represent difficultly organized ecosystem, wherein variables of Input parameters — the factors of development — into obtained variables of Output parameters — the activity results — are being transformed. On the basis of the DEA, data distribution matrix by categories: resources, results, inflexible parameters,- will be built and conclusions on regional culture industries effectiveness will be obtained. DEA-analysis will help to determine the vector of constructive solution search in management system, during indicative plans work-out and control functions implementation; this non-parametric method of the evaluation of operating units group will make it possible to clarify the most effective their groups that is important in the course of strategic planning of culture industry regional strategies and allows to respond more rapidly to new information and to implement regional policies more effectively. All applied methods are substantiated by strict proofs, and baseline data for economic development indicators analysis will be shown.

For to develop methodological approaches to regional policy implementation in culture industries regional systems and to improve their efficiency, the SWOT-analysis of strategic directions of this sector development will be used.

For to create program complex, modern programming languages (C#/Java) will be used. For to provide users' access to the results of program processing of data being analyzed, modern graphic interfaces will be exploited which embody visual interface of ending results output:

- creation of research methodology of the culture industry in modern conditions, definition of the industry's determinants, composition, borders and components, their quantitative evaluation in modern conditions;
- characteristics of services market development degree and definition of culture industry development potential across Russia regions;
- new fundamental knowledges on the presence and character of correlation and on the degree of culture industry functioning influence on Russia economic growth according to 2000-2017 data; indicators system, algorithm and evaluation methodology of culture industry influence on RF regions' economic growth;
- regions' classification methodology work-out, charting of Russia regions' ranking map versus culture industry development level;
- Russia regions' ranking composition for the evaluation of integratedness and efficiency degree of culture industry development;
- evaluation methodology of culture industry regional systems' efficiency and methodology's application algorithm on the grounds of DEA (data envelopment analysis) providing for juxtaposition of efficiency Input parameters and regional culture industries' outcome across Russia regions;
- organizational-economic mechanism of culture industry development in RF regions in the form of clusters and integrated service complexes;
- informational-analytical database on culture industry key indicators for substantiation of placement in Russia regions and of integrated service complexes creation in the culture industry;
- financing mechanism of layout activity in the culture sphere on the basis of public-private partnership with the use of integrated service complexes and effective forms development of the partnership organization in the culture sphere;
- integrated service complexes' model concept in the culture industry in Russia regions based on various financing models;

- programming product on analysis and choice of decisions making about culture industry integrated service complexes placement on Russia territory;
- methodical recommendations on culture industry development and organizational support, financing and creation of accompanying institutional environment *in Russian* Federation regions.

Thus, as a result of this project implementation, original new fundamental theoretical provisions and empirical data in the culture industry and regional development field, allowing to determine long-term measures on their effectiveness improvement, will be obtained. It will be analyzed the existing jural, organizational and financial models, organizational and financing forms and mechanisms of the culture industry institutions and same but new ones will be worked out, methodological, organizational, resource, regulatory-legal support of the culture industry will be created.

The project methodological results (development of culture industry research methodology, regions ranking per development level, efficiency analysis and support mechanisms of the culture industry) can be used to assess state policy and legislation (in order to determine the vectors of long-term strategic planning of direct and indirect measures of state support), to work out the regional policy in the culture industry (when determining the integrated service complexes placement, financing, clusterogenesis sources and so on).

The project empirical results allow to carry out a comparative quantitative analysis, to assess synergetic and multiplier effects of the culture industry development in the regional view in order to predict the scenarios of economic development and effective allocation of state resources onto the culture, in order to adjust the development goals in dependence of updated specifics of the culture industry spatial structure.

The methodological elements represent a set of scientific methods characterizing the process of microeconomic systems logistization from different aspects. The given elements consist of foundational theories and concepts: systems theories, theory of economy, cybernetics and mathematics, of human capital, theory of optimal functioning, decision-making, project management, as well as of concepts of socio-economic development of the country and regions, of concepts of federal, regional and corporate policy in the field of the culture sphere service (Fig. 2.1).

Regulatory-legal elements of organizational-economic mechanism is an effective way of the logistization process regulating since they are

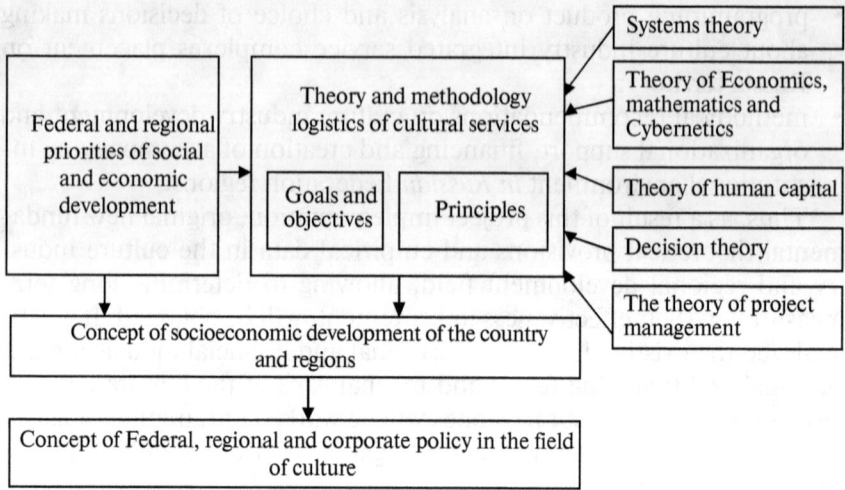

Figure 2.1. Methodological elements of the organizational and economic mechanism of logistics of the sphere of culture

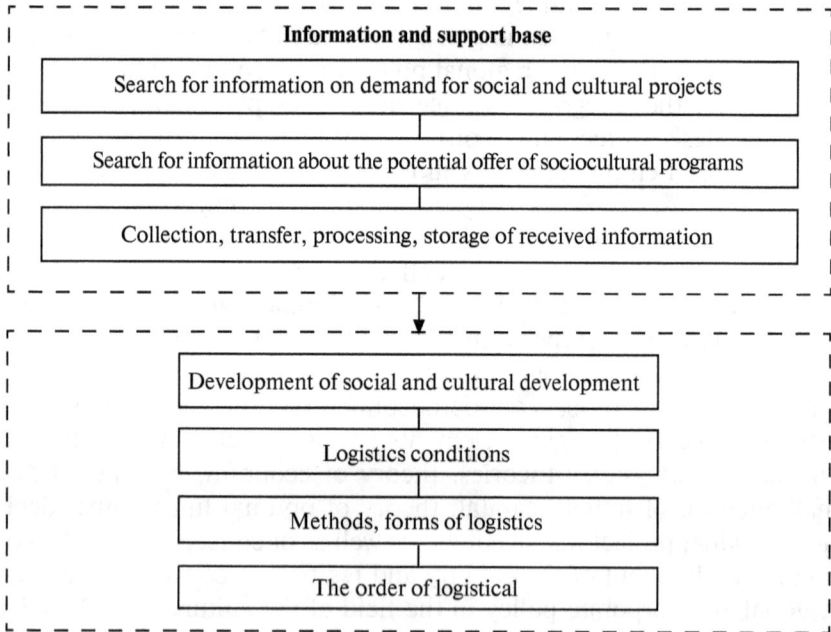

Figure 2.2. Information and methodological elements of the organizational and economic mechanism of logistics

capable at greater extent to synthesize the possibilities of regulating the relations between participants (subjects) arising in the course of the given process. The process of system logistization of the culture sphere services cannot be effective without informational support (information collection, transmission, processing and storage) per various stages of this process as well as without the development of methodological basis for its implementation.

Therefore, informational-methodological elements should be formed. They assume informational support of the logistization process as well as — strictly certain, consecutive order of its implementation (Fig. 2.2).

The methodological framework implies the work-out of projects for the culture sphere services system logistization that adds in definition of goals, participants, conditions, methods, means and order of the process. Informational-methodological elements constitute a block of means of influence on the management of social-cultural programs.

The block of means of the impact on resource provision of organizational-economic mechanism presupposes the existence of economic-financial elements since in its frames, required financial resources volume, their sources of influx, regulation of funds movemen, logistization budget are determined, efficiency and risk assessment are pursued (Fig. 2.3).

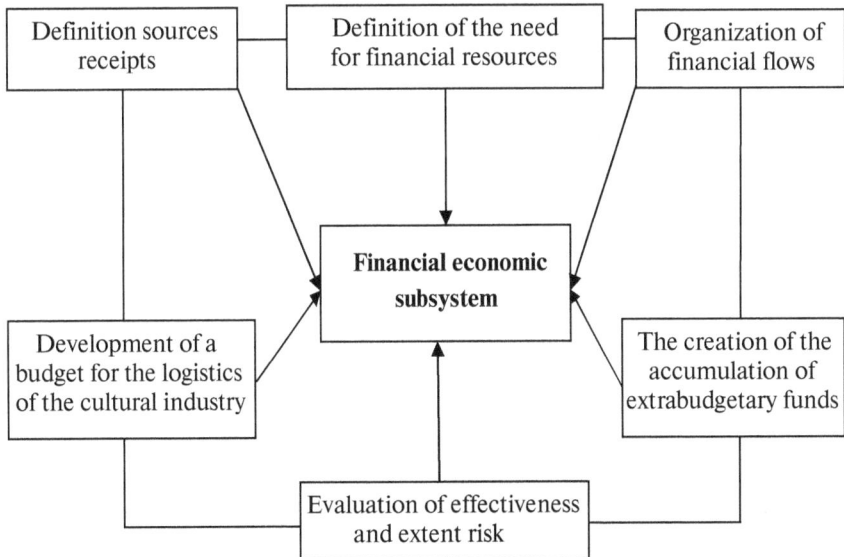

Figure 2.3. Financial and economic elements of the organizational and economic mechanism of logistics of the system of services of the industry of culture

The managemental elements assume regulation of mutual relations between participants of logistization process of the culture sphere services system (Fig. 2.4). The given elements have their content as definition of purposes, tasks, functions and responsibility of each participant of the process, and also of principles and interaction schemes of all subjects of the organizational-economic mechanism.

Thus, organizational-economic mechanism of the culture sphere services system logistization has a complex structure consisting of modules, blocks and elements. The modules are divided according to the directions in respect of individual groups of micro-economic systems. The blocks — are parts of the mechanism determining the influence ways row by management system different trends. The blocks consist of elements which represent individual means, models and methods of influence on the management system.

The participants of the logistization process, the consequences of their interaction in this process, the goals, task forms facing each participant are defined. The principles of participants interaction as well as the incentives of their effective participation in the process are worked out. The functions of state, business structures and public organizations in the course of their interaction are defined.

All elements of the organizational-economic mechanism of the logistization of the culture sphere services system are closely interrelated and interact being in a single system. To determine the result of the culture sphere services system logistization, it is necessary on the strength of supposed, being fulfilled functions to hold an analysis of resource capacities and provision means and to open up interaction of logistizationsubjects and objects and, by providing services range, generated by service flows, to solve initial goals and objectives. The interaction of the mechanism elements constitutes its content and ensures its self-regulation.

The results application of the current study in the form of large-scale creation and application in practice of the integrated service complexes, as well as of financing mechanisms on the terms of public-private partnership has a high applied importance and will allow:
- to expand the culture institutions client database through the development of new segments of the culture industry services market which will increase the volume of consumption of the pursued services and the incomes of the culture industry subjects on the basis of integration;
- to provide citizens for the demanded services, to develop the culture industry infrastructure;

- to reduce expenditures and logistic costs of the industry;
- to optimize the state budget expenditures on the formation and development of the culture industry services through the use of public-private partnerships in this area;
- to create favorable conditions for attracting investment into services sphere in a whole and in the culture industry;
- to reduce the risk degree of entering of new consumer markets of culture industry services sphere;
- to increase the cost-effectiveness of the culture industry functioning by providing an open access to information and main characteristics of the culture services.

Comparison of the project obtained results with modern foreign research results will allow to demonstrate the results as corresponding ones to the world level.

The necessary restructuring of the culture sector begins from the identification of the culture institutions which are ready-to-operate on a market basis, and of culture institutions, providing for the services on a non-market basis. In the first group (operating on market conditions), the author proposes to transform ones into integrated service complexes, to expand the rights of resource flow management, the range of paid services and the regulation of revenues from them. Financing of this group services is recommended to be carried out within the frames of public-private partnership, project financing, program-target support and others. In the second group (of non-market basis), ones remain as part of state guaranteed financing. The given actions introduction satisfies in the fullest way the demands for a diverse cultural life of society without burdening the state budget with additional expenses in the culture field.

The formation of attractive conditions for finances in the culture industry increases the competitiveness of the services and the works sector as well as of the integration processes each participant at the development each stage and level. The integration of creative industry and consciousness industry into economic relations by the way of the integrated service complexes introduction should proceed in two stages [5]. On the first stage, the indicators of the constituent industries: economic, social and cultural ones- are calculated. On the second one — the effectiveness of the subject's industry in a whole.

On the present stage, it is possible to distinguish the main models of the creative industry financing: regulatory budget, program-target, project, endowment-fund, commercial hiring, rent, leasing ones etc. The need to abandon the estimated funding and to expand the economic independence has manifested itself plainly in practice during a long time period so far.

Based on the world experience of the application of culture financing different models (the USA — sponsorship and fundraising, the Great Britain — PPP (Public-Private Partnership) mechanism). Usage of the principles of the culture services funding on PPP basis possesses the characteristic feature of innovational activity: the presence of scientific-technical novelty — the ensuring of structural relationship between formation different links, the promotions and sales of the culture services as well as the ensuring of end-to-end management of material, financial and accompanying flows with the help of the latest informational technologies that will increase the spread of services active kinds on the culture industry market.

Concession and quasi-concession schemes can be considered today as possible mechanisms of cooperation in the creative industry. Among the PPP mechanisms, there are applicable to innovative projects in the creative industry- Life Cycle Contracts (LCC) — concessions DBFM (Design Build Finance Maintain). Under the LCC terms, an investor designs and creates an object at his own expense, and then exploits it throughout a lifecycle, carrying out repairs and maintenance, the state pays for the services provided with the help of such object. The state establishes functional requirements for the object within the LCC frames. The investor ensures that the object meets these requirements throughout the contract. If the investor does not fulfill his obligations under the contract or does not fulfill them properly, the payment is terminated. Time terms of LC contracts correspond to the terms of economically conditioned exploitation of infrastructure facility. LC contracts mechanism can be effective towards galleries and museums.

Alike agreements would allow to make capital investments into fixed assets of the culture institutions which are experiencing a budget deficit and, at the same time, have commercial attractiveness for investors. Abroad, the concession scheme has already proved its practical effectiveness. When using the LC contract the state starts funding from project start time and continues annually with mandatory control of simple and estimated performance criteria.

The development of endowments in Russia is directed to promoting an endowment model as an effective tool for activities financing of non-profit organizations in the culture sphere. The formation of regional "growth points" on the basis of endowments and the subsequent multiplier effect for regional and national economies is one of the most important macroeconomic tasks. Endowment-fund is not only an additional source of culture industry income but it also becomes an indicator of competitiveness through integration with universities' scientific potential. Analysis of the experience of the endowment-funds has allowed to determine their major characteristics, successful functioning factors in Russia and financing development directions of the culture and creativity sphere as well as of education sphere via the endowment funds.

Major tools of public-private partnership in the culture industries may be legal, organizational and financial forms, and major models — methodological, organizational, resource, regulatory-legal and motivational support. The directions of public-private partnership usage are quite extensive: state and political patronage, organizational-economic and investing-financial conditions, regulatory-jural base, human resourcing.

The culture industry support for and the formation of organizational-economic mechanism for managing the given process are particularly vital for the Russian economy because of the presence of significant untapped reserves, potential opportunities for the effective application of logistic approach and of integrating strategies formation.

Financing methods of innovative design in the culture field are possible as a technology to maintain the cultural services' variety, their market demand boost that allows to embody tight dependence of financing purpose from activities results. Main directions of the reform of culture services' backing system — are inter-industries and inter-budgetary relations of the culture sphere in the frames of various activity kinds.

Based on the usage analysis of tools of endowment, public-private partnership, guarantee schemes and other financial-credit mechanisms and innovative funding tools in the culture industry, the concept of integrated service complexes models in the culture industry is masterminded as a mechanism for development and support of the culture industry in Russia regions, grounded on backing different models.

Application of the current study results in the form of large-scale creation and in the form of financing mechanisms introduction is of high applied significance and that will allow:
- to expand culture institutions client contacts on the backs of market new segments development of the culture services industry which will enhance consumption volume of held services and of culture industry subjects' income on integration basis;
- to provide citizens with demanded services, to develop the culture industry infrastructure;

- to optimize the state budget expenditures towards the culture industry services formation and development from public-private partnership utilization in this sphere;
- to create favorable conditions for investments attracting into services sphere in a whole and into the culture industry;
- to reduce the risk degree of entry of the culture industry services into consumer's new markets;
- to heighten the profitability of the culture industry functioning by the way of providing an open access to culture services information and major characteristics.

REFERENCE LIST

1. Bourbieu P. Field of Cultural Production: Essays on Art and Literature // *R. Jonson. Cambridge: Polity press* 1993, p. 21.
2. Throsby D. Economics and Culture // *M. Ed. House. Higher School of Economics.* 2013, p. 159 *(in Russian)*.
3. Benjamin V. Work of Art in the Era of its Technical Reproducibility // *Moscow: Goethe Cultural Center; Medium* 1996. p. 196 *(in Russian)*.
4. Adorno T. W. Culture Industry Reconsidered, in Culture Industry // R. W. Witkin, Adorno on Popular Culture, p. 85.
5. Malshina N.A. Model of Management Improvement of Flow Processes in Integrated Services Complexes // Saratov University News. New series. Series "Economics. Management. Right" 2014. No. 1. pp. 163–167 *(in Russian)*.

3. LOGISTICS AS ACTUALIZATION OF SOCIAL-CULTURAL SERVICES INNOVATIVE POTENTIAL

At the moment in Russia, positive dynamics of services proportion comes out in more than 50% of GDP. In European developed countries, according to statistics, about 70% of GDP is produced in services sector, and the growth rate is 16% per year, compared to the trade sector — 7% per year [13].

The modern market economy of the developed world countries functions as an economy of services sphere. Starting from C20th second half of the twentieth and C21th beginning, one of the market relations main trends is the rapid expansion of the services sphere. Modern level of developed countries economy demonstrates the services market dynamic development. Among the leading sectors of the world economy, the culture sphere occupies one of the first places in terms of created jobs number and, hence, in terms of impact on dynamics and structure of consumption spending and investments. However, the culture sphere demands constant financial support from the state side.

Activities in the culture field ensure at present the growth of indicators on socio-economic criteria of either individual regions or the industry branch in a whole. The first European study conducted in 1984 in Zurich was devoted to "the economic significance of Zurich culture institutions" [15]. Based on the study of the culture sector financial flows of the city of Zurich, it was established that "26.2% of state subsidies being directed to the culture sector are directly or indirectly returning to the state that is causing a strong revitalizing effect on the economy" [15].

The assessment of the economic output of the culture and art sphere showed that "the culture and art sphere creates jobs for 12 thousand people that constitutes 1.6% of the city residents" [15]. As previously noted by European researchers, "among 48 leading sectors of Amsterdam's economy, the culture sector ranks eighth by the number of jobs created that is ahead of the advertising and newspaper-publishing businesses" [15]. In the 1990s, in Europe, the culture sphere activities had begun to be used to attract investments into crisis subjects, to create jobs.

In RF, on May 2017, "the population was provided for paid services with 705.6 billion rubles, on January-May 2017 — with 3521.3 billion rubles. Expenditures share for the services sphere payments amidst population consumption expenses on May 2017 amounted to 21.3% (on May 2016. — 21,4%)" [14].

The analysis of the world experience on functioning testifies to maximal efficiency of integrated logistical service both in micro-and macro-economic terms. While meeting this condition, the logistical companies (providers, operators) ensure complex diversified logistical services on promotion and maintenance of resource flows. "Composite of infrastructure facilities, located on the local territory, where integration and coordination of mainly operational logistical activities is implemented, has been named abroad as a logistical center" [7]. The logistical center is considered in the current situation in the world practice as a "spatial-functional object together with infrastructure and managing organization which logistical services, connected with goods transportation, acceptance, storage, distribution and delivery as well as related services provided by independent towards owner or recipient business-conducting entities, are embodied in" [2].

In our opinion, main principles of logistical management of socio-cultural sphere organization in the modern conditions are in construction of flexible and adaptive organizational structures as well as the wide use of situational approach in the management according to which a state of organization internal environment constitutes a response to external factors impact. Clarifying our point in this matter, we would like to note that external factors influence development has drastically increased at the modern stage for the reason of complication, crisis condition of all of the system of public relations (legal, social, political, economic and so on). Namely external situation today in the crisis conditions dictates management strategy and tactics of the socio-cultural sphere.

Of course, with unconditional significance of external factors, the achievement of strategic objectives and the successful holding tactical events largely depend on activities self-internal conditions: perfection degree of structural-functional complex, efficiency of activities forms and method as well as state of resource base of socio-cultural sphere.

Modern socio-cultural services sphere as an open socio-economic system is characterized by signs of integrity, i.e. dynamic interaction of its components is defined by the presence of common goals for to achieve which the sphere is being created, the sphere objectively depends on the external environment state, possesses the adaptation property and strives to find the balance between the internal capabilities and the external environment for to maintain its steady state.

The logistical methods application in previously unused areas is due to the development of integration processes. At the modern stage, business-structures represent themselves as open systems where the relationships are being built on the principles of mutually beneficial conditions, on the principles of cooperation and outsourcing.

The logistical approaches application is especially feasible if the need displays itself of a quick solution of complicated informational and optimization tasks implying an orientation to market strategy as a whole one rather than on particular links of the logistical chain.

The effectiveness of management logistical methods is in the change of strategic work complex economic results as a key condition of business-structures competitiveness.

Logistical centers (LC) concept began to actualize in 1980s, "providing companies with a range of services and representing itself as structures which frames within several companies-operators, carry out complex logistical activities on a commercial basis; the activities target both international and domestic transportation" [16]. The introduction of LC networks along the main Eurasian transport routes "addresses costs reduction of export and import deliveries, comprehensive services while crossing borders, transport downtime cut at customs control points as well as on inventories decline in transit and at shippers and consignees facilities" [17].

In the field of international transport infrastructure development and formation of LC network, "EU countries are guided by the existing recommendations of the European Commission" [5] that provides for the functioning of backbone European LC.

It is confirmed on the basis of results of research projects and practical actions of European companies that "LC can play a significant role in the support of intermodality and create an incentive for a shift towards multimodal transportations in the global supply chains linking the countries joining the European Union and the European Union current members" [3, p. 32]. In this aspect, LC main objectives in the EU are:
- "attracting of large private investments into LC project actualization" [11];
- "construction of high-tech production-warehouse facilities and integrated infrastructure of roadside service" [11];
- "creation of up-to-date and effective systems of engineering, communicational and informational maintenance of LC" [11];
- introduction of modern informational technologies functioning in accordance with international standards and regulations;
- "improvement of customs inspection procedures, of goods and vehicles registration and control, bringing them into line with world practice" [11];

- consolidation of freight forwarding companies on goods delivery due to the need for informational networking and terminal technologies in LC;
- "creation of an effective distribution network of LC for developing large retail structures and networks as well as stores-warehouses of wholesale and small wholesale selling of import production groceries, focused on revival and legalization of trade-procurement business of private enterprises" [11].

"The complex of performed functions by LC being created in Europe allows to consider them not only in a role of national transport-logistical hubs but also as a kind of peculiar framework, cementing transportation process, rolling-stock and infrastructure into a single integrated system not only of the country and/or the EU region but also into a global market in the perspective" [4].

In the countries of world economic leaders, "LC, carrying out complex (3PL) services related to transportation, warehousing and cargo processing (for consignments consolidation and unbundling, transshipment, forwarding, storage), goods customs clearance, cargo insurance, warehouse inventory management, calculation-payment operations, informational-analytical services of shippers and consignees" have been created and been effectively operating [2, p. 22]. The packages of provided services by them may include logistical consulting, engineering, marketing, informational services and other 4PL-level services. Often, "4PL providers in the West act as LC management companies" [18].

Studies of German scientists in 2008–2010 demonstrated that 50% of local entities, exploiting transportation and distributions LCs, are going to abandon their own transport-warehouse infrastructure in near future. The examples can be: "macrologistical projects of LC networks creation implemented in the period of 1990–2004: "Collomodul", "Germes", TACIS 95 [20], TEDIM, INTERREGIII B and some others" [15]. In the developing countries, first of all in the EurAsEU (Eurasion Economic Union) countries, "the external effect of LC networks formation has not been yet too noticeable" [19]. However, transnational logistical companies are increasingly entering these markets and are rapidly becoming the dominant force in transport and logistics sphere that will inevitably affect jobs and working conditions in these countries. Because of market trends the necessity has been appearing to clarify the range of the most utilized definitions of "logical center" term. Just it is the reminder that there is no publicly accepted classification of LC currently which would require an obligatory revision. "A logistics center — is a geographical association of independent companies and enterprises being engaged in freight transport (e.g. transport intermediaries, shippers, transport operators, customs authorities) and related services (e.g. on storage, technical maintenance and repairment) including one terminal, at least" [8, p. 4] — it is a consolidated definition of United Nations Economic Commission for Europe (UNECE), European Conference of Ministers of Transport (ECMT) and European Commission (EC), 2001. "Logistics center — is a centre on a definite territory within which operations related to transportation and other logistical functions as well as goods distribution — for both national and international transit — are carried out by several operators on a commercial basis." The definition of "NeLoC project participants " [9, p. 44], LC should operate "in accordance with European standards, also including quality standards, to provide a basis for commercial, balanced transport solutions, EU programs of INTER-REGIII B and TEDIM" [10]. "Logistics center — is a spatial-functional object together with an infrastructure and a management organization, which logistics services are actualized in, related to the transportation, acceptance, storage, distribution and delivery of goods, as well as accompanying services provided by economic entities that are independent towards a sender or recipient" [1, p. 24]. Hence, LC is considered as a structure uniting several companies functioning as a complex logistical company.

Under necessity of logical center concept application, the transformation takes place in the culture sphere in the form of an "integrated service complex considered as a complicated multifunctional system including a set of productions, processes, material devices on the creation of the culture industry services and their production, distribution and consumption" [6, p. 185].

Calculation of economic efficiency indicators of culture institutions activity should be made according to the established indicators:

"The average price of one visit to a paid event in Cultural-Leisure Institution (CLI), "[7] in thousands of rubles, is calculated by the formula:

$$P_{vis} = \frac{\left(\dfrac{A_m}{E_p}\right)}{\left(\dfrac{V_{sub}}{E_p}\right)},$$

where P_{vis} — average price of a one visit to CLI, in thousand rubles; A_m — obtained for a year from mainstream statutory activities, in thousand rubles; Ep — number of cultural-leisure events on a paid basis, in numbers;

V_{sub} — visitors number of paid cultural-leisure events in a territorial subject of RF in a reporting year, in persons. [7]

"Share of CLI expenditures coverage by incomes from mainstream types of statutory activity,%%," [7] is calculated by formula:

$$SEC = \frac{A_m + Ae}{C} \cdot 100\%,$$

where SEC — share of CLI Expenditures Coverage by incomes from mainstream types of statutory activity, %%; A_m — obtained for a year from mainstream statutory activities, in thousand rubles; A_e — obtained for a year from entrepreneurship activities, in thousand rubles; C — CLI costs for a year, in thousand rubles. [7]

"Attendance of paid cultural-leisure events" [7] conducted by state and municipal culture institutions in a reporting year, in numbers, is calculated by formula:

$$V = \frac{V_{sub}}{N_{av}},$$

where V — paid attendance of cultural-leisure events held by state (municipal) culture institutions in a reporting year, in numbers; V_{sub} — visitors number of paid cultural-leisure events in territorial subject of RF in a reporting year, in persons; N_{av} — mid-year population of Russian Federation territorial subject in a reporting year, in persons." [7]

"Attendance of paid cultural-leisure activities" [7] held by state (municipal) culture institutions in previous reporting year, in numbers, is calculated by formula:

$$V_1 = \frac{V_{pre}}{V'_{pre}},$$

where V_1 — paid attendance at cultural-leisure events held by state (municipal) culture institutions in a previous reporting year, in numbers; V_{pre} — number of visitors of paid cultural-leisure events in RF subject in a previous reporting year, in persons; V'_{pre} — mid-year permanent population of Russian Federation territorial subject, in persons [7].

"Attendance dynamics of paid cultural-leisure events" [12], conducted by state and municipal culture institutions in a reporting year in relation to a previous year,%%, is calculated by formula:

$$D_a = \frac{V}{V_1} \cdot 100\%,$$

where D_a — attendance dynamics of paid cultural-leisure events held by state (municipal) cultural institutions, %%; V — paid attendance of cultural-leisure events held by state (municipal) culture institutions, in persons; V_1 — paid attendance of cultural-leisure events held by state (municipal) culture institutions in a previous reporting year, in numbers [7].

"The share of socially significant cultural-leisure events versus total number of held events in a reporting year,%%," [12] is calculated by formula:

$$E_{soc} = \frac{\left(E \dfrac{C_{soc}}{C} \right)}{E},$$

where E_{soc} — share of socially important cultural-leisure events versus total number of events held in a reporting year,%; E — number of cultural-leisure events in a reporting year; C_{soc} — CLI costs of socially significant events in a reporting year, in thousand rubles [12].

The logistic potential of the culture industry should be calculated in accordance with definition and according to function indicator, the potential should be as reflecting the ability of enterprise functioning upon maximal results achievement at minimal costs. The overall strategic competitive potential is expressed in the form:

$$L_{ket} = \prod_{t=1}^{\bar{t}} L_t,$$

where L_{ket} — multiplication of individual, t, potentials of enterprise; L_t — numerical assessment of individual competitive potential of t-type enterprise; t — type of enterprise individual potential.

The most important factor determining the managing peculiarity of organization of the socio-cultural sphere in the post-crisis and crisis conditions is a sharp acceleration of risk degree. It is predetermined, first of all, by the high uncertainty of arranging circumstances in the external environment.

While modernizing the management of business structures of social-cultural services, it is of primary importance to take into account the peculiarities of the services provided because it is namely them which largely determine the structure and objectives of the management subsystem. It seems necessary to build the organizational-economic mechanism of this process in accordance with the principle of orientation to the development of relevant business structures [6, p. 57] (Fig. 3.1).

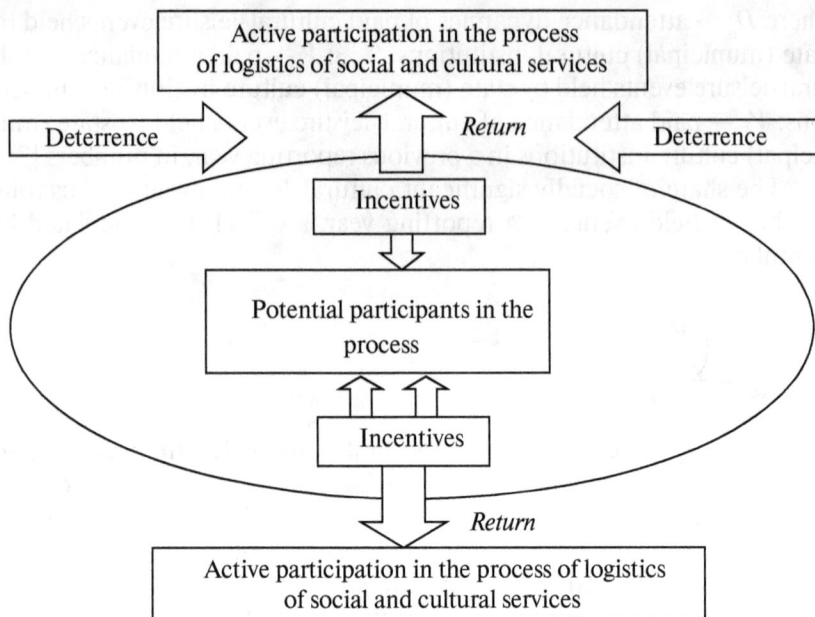

Figure 3.1. The principle of economic stimulation of participation
and restraint in the process of logistics of socio-cultural services

The development of microeconomic systems together should be characterized by quantitative and qualitative positive changes of its parameters (of functional, administrative, social and service subsystems). This has a concrete implication in the quantitative and qualitative growth of the service system, in the increase of the qualitive level of the process of formation, completion of the services package, labor activity activation as well as in income boost and investment capital attraction.

The results of the implementation of this principle is, at macro- and meso-economic level, the development of national and regional socio-cultural services complex, market development of socio-cultural services, meeting the social needs of the community.

The use of logistic methods for integrated business processes should be one of the most important goals for the formation of Russia socio-cultural services system. Long-term logistic partnership in services socio-cultural sphere is preferable for the following reasons: it allows to create sustainable channels of advanced knowledge transfer; modern organizational and technological breakthroughs, including logistic ones, are formed at the junction of sciences or industries; joint developments and innovative projects allow to reduce the costs and risks of the integration process. In this case, trust stands as an economic factor providing a balance between the development and competitive advantages for all participants of the socio-cultural services logistic system. Targeting principle is at the basis of practical implementation fundamental of logistic methods of culture field management, the principle implies to identify activities trends relatively separate groups of microeconomic systems depending on the needs in specific services and their implementation within particular models (Fig. 3.2).

This principle implies also the development of state guarantees system of culture sphere services.

Bearing the offered principles, the basis for effectiveness assessment of management of culture sphere business-structures in the crisis conditions with the help of logistic methods will be:
• to determine measuring instruments;
• verification of measuring instruments practical implementation;

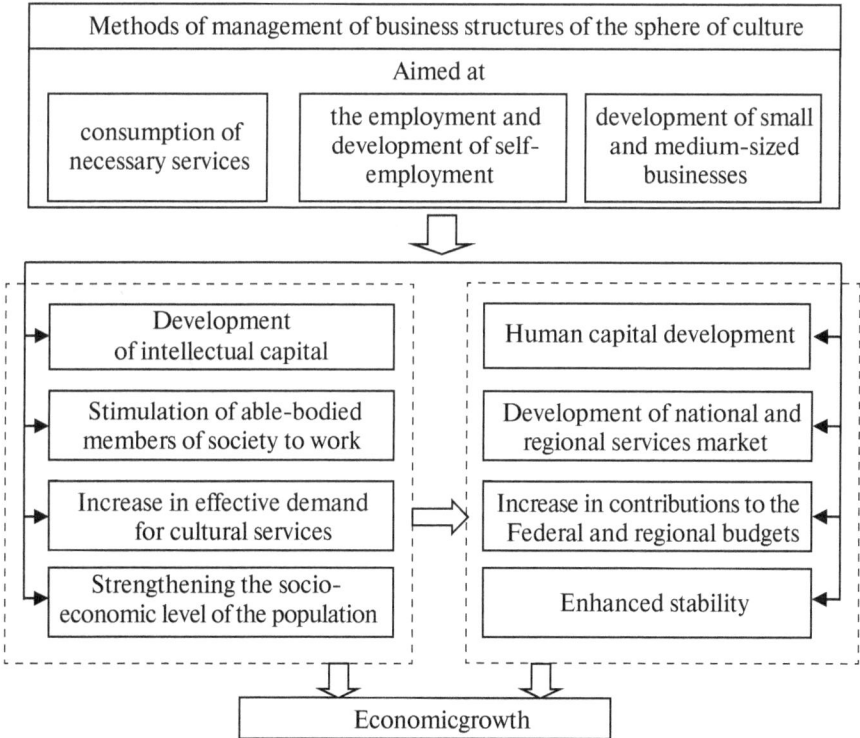

Figure 3.2. The principle of orientation for the development of the culture sphere

- conditions creation for to use functioning efficiency concise indicators;
- evaluation of the obtained coefficients and indices in accordance with logistic system functioning criteria.

The activities results find direct reflection in the value of actual expenses associated with the implementation of operational tasks. The definition of expected expenses is the essence of budget planning. The value of logistic expenses is expressed either by the total monetary amount of costs or by the monetary amount calculated per production unit (i.e. costs per unit), or by a share in the volume of sales.

Effective functioning and sustainable development of the culture sphere institution requires the forecasting of difficulties as well as of new opportunities. Business-structures of the culture sphere institution today settle tasks complex of strategic planning and development.

Strategic planning methods usage presupposes innovative activities, business-processes logistization, structural-functional and other changes necessary to adapt to external environment impacts.

Insufficient clearness of the culture sphere institution further development at present stage is due to the lack of timely reliable information about the character of ongoing economic processes in Russia, about measures of consequences overcoming of the crisis and foreign countries anti-Russian sanctions, as well as due to the lack of tested developings on post-crisis condition adaptation.

Russia culture sphere institutions belong to economy branches that constantly interact with international world business, and culture sphere business-structures carry out activity in economic zones of foreign countries, develop world market of goods and services.

The changing logistic potential of an activity subject shows a delayed and weakened response to positive impacts, in contrast to the influence of destructive factors having a rapid effect.

Thus, in the business-structures management of social-cultural services, it is necessary to consider them in the unity and integrity of the components which are inextricably linked to the outside world.

REFERENCE LIST

1. ARTANDHOUSES — URL: http://art-and-houses.ru/2017/07/21/muzejnyj-bum-2017/.
2. Gabler — Lexicon on Logistics. Logistic Management. Terms and Definitions. Text // Under editorship of Professor P. Clauss, Professor V. Krieger. Germany, Weisbaden, Gabler Publishing house, 2000. — 449 p.

3. Garnov A.P., Kireeva N.S. Financial, Material and Information Flows: Point of Interaction in Logistics // RISK: Resources, Information, Supply, Competition. — 2017. — No. 2. 48–51 pp. *(in Russian)*.
4. Garnov A., Kireeva N. Strategic Planning and Management as a Basis for Increasing by Multi-Link Logistic Chains of Business Cost // Logistics. — 2012. No. 1 (62). 20–23 pp. *(in Russian)*.
5. Logistics Efficiency Index for 2016 / Logistic Portal. — URL: https://www.lobanov-logist.ru/library/353/63185/ *(in Russian)*.
6. Malshina N.A. Conceptual Functioning Principles of Organizational-Economic Mechanism of Socio-cultural Service System // LogistizationVestnikUniversiteta. — No. 5. — 2013, 48–62 pp. *(in Russian)*.
7. Sergeev V.I. General Trends in the Development of Logistic Centers Abroad // Scientific-analytical journal "Logistics and Supply Chain Management". — October 2012 № 5 (52) — URL: http://www.lscm.ru/index.php/ru/avtoram/item/1177 *(in Russian)*.
8. Federal State Statistics Service — URL: http://www.gks.ru/wps/wcm/connect/rosstat_main/rosstat/ru/statistics/enterprise/retail/#*(in Russian)*.
9. Garnov A., Protsenko I. Vital Problems of Logistic Management of Cargo Transportation Processes // RISK: Resources, Information, Supply, Competition. 2016. No. 2. — 30–33 pp. *(in Russian)*.
10. European Agreement on the Most Important International Combined Transport Lines and Related Facilities (AGTC). Accepted in Geneva February 1 1991 http://docs.cntd.ru/document/901855484 (accessed on June 12, 2017).
11. Logistics Efficiency Index for 2016. Logistic Portal. — URL: https://www.lobanov-logist.ru/library/353/63185/ *(in Russian)*.
12. Malshina N.A. Integrated Service Complex of Culture Industry in Subjects of the Russian Federation // Izvestiya Saratov University. New series: Economics. Management.Right. — 2016. — No. 2.180-186pp. *(in Russian)*.
13. RF Ministry of Culture Order of June 28, 2013 N 920 "On approval of methodical recommendations on developing by public authorities of Russian Federation subjects and local governments of activity efficiency indicators of subordinated culture institutions, their heads and workers by the institution types and workers main categories" — URL: http://www.garant.ru/products/ipo/prime/doc/70327762/#ixzz4nejrFzSc (accessed on June 12, 2017, *in Russian*).
14. TACIS-95 program: Development of Transport Sector in the Russian Federation: North-West Transport Corridor. — Brussels: "TACIS", 1995. 24p.

15. Prokofieva T.A., Sergeev V.I. Logistical Centers in the Transport System of Russia: Textbook // Ed. house "Economic Newspaper", 2012, 524 p. *(in Russian)*.
16. Sergeev V.I. Conceptual Approaches for Design and Classification of Logistic Centers // Logistics and Supply Chain Management. 2010. No. 4. 8–19 pp. *(in Russian)*.
17. Sergeev V.I. General Trends of the Development of Logistics Centers Abroad // Scientific-analytical journal. Logistics and Supply Chain Management 2012. No. 5 (52). URL: http://www.lscm.ru/index.php/ru/ (accessed on June 12, 201, *in Russian*).
18. System of Indicators to Assess the Effectiveness of State Theater. // Handbook of Culture Institution Head. — 2016, — No. 8. — URL: http://vip.1cult.ru/# (accessed on June 12, 2017, *in Russian*).
19. Socio-economic Situation of Russia — 2017 // Federal State Statistics Service — URL: http://www.gks.ru/bgd/regl/b17_01/Main.htm (accessed on June 12, 2017, *in Russian*).
20. Federal State Statistics service — URL: http://www.gks.ru/wps/wcm/connect/rosstat_main/rosstat/ru/statistics/enterprise/retail/# (accessed on June 12, 2017, *in Russian*).
21. ARTANDHOUSES-URL: http://art-and-houses.ru/2017/07/21/muzejnyj-bum-2017/ (accessed on June 12, 2017).
22. Bowersox D.J., Kloss D.J., Gelferich O.K. Logistical Management // Macmillan Publishers, 3., 1991.
23. Exploring the Northern Dimension — URL: http://www.ndinstitute.org (accessed on June 12, 2017).
24. Private Participation in Infrastructure Projects Database. The World Bank Group — The Public-Private Infrastructure Advisory Faculty July 2008.
25. TNS Media Research. — URL: http://www.ilctraceca.org (accessed on June 12, 2017).

4. RESEARCH OF METHODOLOGICAL TOOLS OF CREATIVE INDUSTRY LOGISTIZATION PROCESS

During the analysis of RF culture industry as one of the elements of service sector, overall negative dynamics of its development is being confirmed over the last long period of time. However, stable positive dynamics of some indicators of CI development is being observed. Thus, "... share of total expenditures of the consolidated budget of the Russian Federation has negative trend in the structure of expenditures on cultural services for 1991–2014 period and had reached its maximum of 1.89% in 2005, and year 2013 was marked by slight increase of expenditures on culture and cinematography, and the positive dynamics of up to 1.47% continued in 2014–2017" [1].

There is a stable trend of increase in the volume of services production by 0.3% in Quarter 1 (January-March) of 2019 compared to Quarter 4 (October-December) of 2018 in EU countries by 2019 beginning. A monthly Index of Services (IoS) decreased by 0.1% in the period from February 2019 to March 2019. Figure 4.1 shows IoS for the quarter and the wholesale, retail and automotive sector index with account of seasonal fluctuations for the period from Quarter 1 of 2015 to Quarter 1 of 2019.

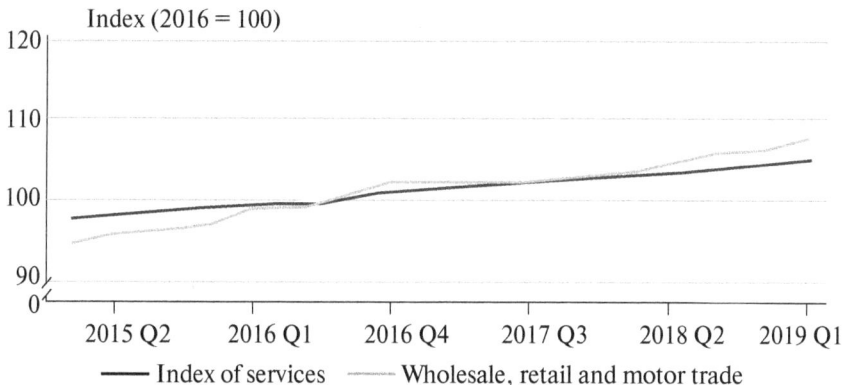

Figure 4.1. Services production volume increased by 0.3% in Quarter 1 (January-March) of 2019. Source: national Statistics Authority — services index https://www.gov.uk

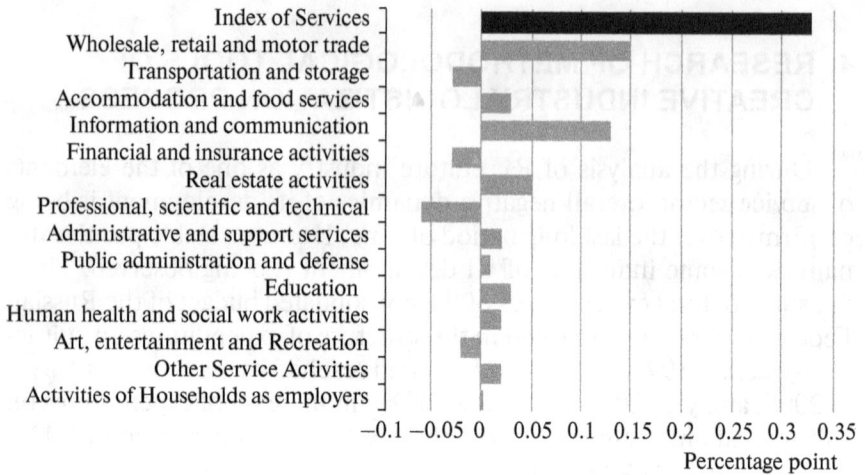

Figure 4.2. Contribution to quarterly services growth with account of seasonal fluctuations, the Great Britain, quarter 1 (January — March) of 2019 [2]

As it is seen from Great Britain official statistics, the contribution of the services sector into GDP is constantly increasing (Figure 4.2). The creative industry as an integral part of the service sector is also showing positive dynamics. From January to March of 2019, there were a total of 11.6 million visits to museums and galleries. This is an increase of 3.0% (about 324,000 visits) compared to the same period in 2018. All museums and galleries are subject to seasonal fluctuations in the number of visits. General tendency is in that the number of visits will be higher during school holidays. Some temporary exhibitions attract a large number of visitors, and this will also affect monthly indexes. There may also be the cases when all museum or gallery or their part is closed for repairs that affects the monthly total.

Basing on multiyear European and world development experience in a whole, one can affirm that the creative industry is the centers of mass consumers' attraction. The flow of consumers' attracted funds has a rapid turnover and, hence, brings a tangible and rapid income. Global mechanism for resource flow management in the creative industry has not been applied and requires adaptation to Russian practice. There are no state and political structures and traditions in the RF which could incorporate successfully into these new systems. A certain vacuum has been appearing in the matters of relationships between state, business, science and culture.

In the world economy, there have been already proven and been bringing stable and increasing income mechanisms and organizational models of the creative industry functioning and management. Flow processes management in the creative industry is quite innovative organizational-economic mechanism for Russia requiring further study and adaptation.

For to study, analyze and evaluate the effectiveness of the flow processes management, for to identify unused resources and for their implementation, for to determine development level and readiness of market system structures for transformations and end-to-end optimization conduct it is required a special scientific tool — an innovative logistics. This logistics corresponds to scientific tool for flow processes' rationalization by introduction of progressive innovations into current and strategic management of the market structures in order to achieve business outcomes [3]. The concept of "logistization process" has been used recently and refers to the field of innovative logistics.

The innovative logistics is aimed at management level increase through the use of innovations various kinds directed towards the improvement of customers' service quality, the efficiency growth of the flow processes and the reduction of their realization total costs.

Therefore, a research object for the innovative logistics are formed flow processes which are, applicably to any public structure activities, the result of management-character measures. Forms and methods of the flow processes management have been becoming an innovative logistics subject which should be improved with the help of the logistic innovations. Despite the tight connection of the innovative logistics by the research object and subject with basic logistics, carrying out daily activities on organization and management of the flow processes of different efficiency degrees, it has its own specific tasks and functions.

The most important component of the innovative logistics is a strategic logistics — a science and practice of the logistic potential extension for various management systems of the flow processes by developing of long-term programs of innovative transformations within planned paradigm of their strategic development.

The strategic orientation in the logistization of service enterprises represents an innovative approach in the flow processes management and has systemic nature that directly can cause a beneficial effect on the enterprises' management and controlling in a whole.

Organizational-economic mechanism of the innovative logistics and its methodological base are specialized structures of innovative logistics service which implement the objective regularity of the modern stage of the market economy. The regularity constitutes further division of labor in all commonweal activities, including scientific ones, as well as in natural activities in the conditions of market globalization, tendency on focus of post-industrial structures' scientific-practical activities on key competencies.

As it is seen, logistization process, in contrast to the logistic approach basic concept, possesses certain innovative characteristics, strategic level of management and functioning. The logistization process necessarily includes not only the activities of market structures on supply management and organization but also the process of development and implementation of the logistics systems of different profiles and levels, the analysis and assessment of necessity and possibility of transformation of existing market structures, i.e. the ability to solve successfully a set of logistic tasks of operational and strategic nature on the flow process optimization.

Distinctive characteristics are more shown as the innovative logistics distinguishes into a special intra-system function or the independent organizations (structures) on logistics service distinguish, providing services on optimal management of material flows not only by delivery participants but also companies with any flow processes (in financial and banking sector; tourism and hospitality; information-communicational sphere and others).

Indeed, the similar characteristics of these concepts exist. These include process goals, objectives, subjects, efficiency evaluation. It is possible to present comparative characteristics of these concepts in a way of Fig. 3.

Analysis and evaluation of the flow process effectiveness in activities different spheres represent the basis and starting point of logistization feasibility, i.e. specific strategic program definition. The program's frames embrace logistic system structure, logistics technology choice, personnel qualification, step-by-step and element-by-element composing of the logistics system, selection of criteria and indicators for program's effectiveness and so on. Herein, the innovative logistics represents those scientific potential which will enable various market structures (which are traditionally oriented, newly created and/or focused on modern forms, methods and technologies of logistics) to work out the logistization program with account of their potential and level of development.

Logistic approach application   **Logistization process**

Similar characteristics

Comprehensive indicators	← Efficiency →	Comprehensive indicatrs
Organizations and participants	← Subjects →	Organizations and participants
Rule «7R»	← Goal →	Rule «7R»

Distinctive characteristic

Basis category	← Category general characteristic →	More innovative category
Activities traditional fields	← Activities field →	Those previously not considered
Traditional resource flows	← Research object →	Flow processes as result of management impact
Optimization of material and related flows	← Research object →	Innovative forms and methods of resource flow management

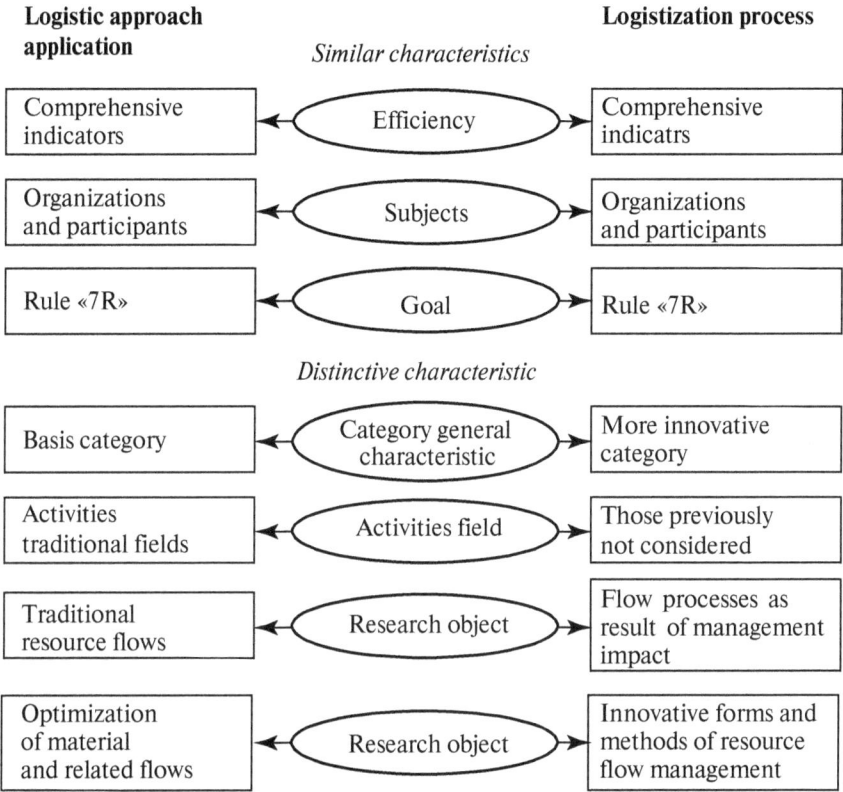

Figure 3. Comparative characteristics of categories
of "application of logistic approach" and "logistization process"

The process of consecutive use of modern logistics (logistics approach) achievements in the management of existing or newly created structures and systems in order to optimize their functioning and development can be called as a logistization process of these structures under condition of meeting the requirements of a "logistics mix" (rule "7R") that is to provide desired product availability in required quantity and of demanded quality in right place at set time for particular consumer with the best costs.

At the same time, a number of scientists avoid this term, assuming that activities in traditionally logistic spheres (branches of production infrastructure) in new market conditions automatically provide a logistic approach, i.e. they are necessarily accompanied by the use of modern logistics achievements (logistics forms, methods, technical tools, advanced information technologies, etc.). However, the spread of sphere of logistic approach application for previously not involved activities areas such as service and tourism, personnel management, innovation, designing and others has become obvious. The use of modern achievements of the logistics in these conditions requires serious preparatory reforms in production, sales, scientific-technical, financial units of domestic enterprises as well as requires adequate internal and external market environment formation. The application of modern logistics tools is either impossible and inefficient without serious changes in domestic structures, otherwise organizational-economic downtime of already arranged simplified (archaic) economic forms and methods of economic management can rise.

Any logistic reforms are accompanied by significant costs and therefore demand the implementation of a consistent and expanded in space and time program of measures that simultaneously represent a complex of necessary socio-economic, organizational-technical, information, legal, staff and other prerequisites for the creation of full-fledged logistic support of the existing structures.

Such a multi-step and, in its essence, innovative process, demanding prolonged and rather expensive experimentation, allows, on the one hand, to carry out comparably even and therefore affordable investing of capital into the logistization process, on the other, to obtain increasing values of annual effect from past and current logistization activities and to compare them with made expenditures.

Measures row in this total program at all stages of its development and realization is the meaning and essence of the logistization. Its content, boundaries, forms, methods and embodiment sequence constitute both spontaneous and purposeful process of spread (introduction) of the logistic approach into the development optimization of the organizational-economic activities.

As a logistization object, both activities traditional spheres, which relate to the logistics ones (production infrastructure) by their nature, or any flow processes, having space-time sequence, can come forward.

The process of logistization can lead to the emergence of the logistic structures wherein activities predominant part proceeds with the use of modern achievements of the logistics and targets an integration and global, from standpoints of the single whole as a system, analytical improvement (rationalization and optimization) of the flow processes with a focus on the final results. Both traditional economic and other structures having undergone the logistization, and structures, being newly created which have been using from the origin in their projection and development the forms and methods of modern logistics, can come forward as logistic structures.

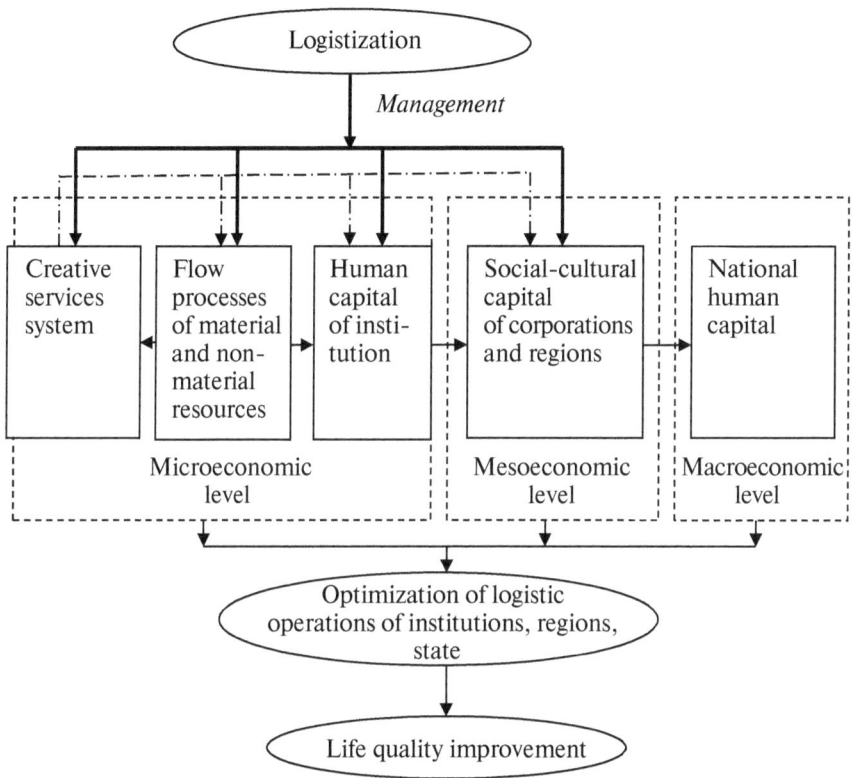

Figure 4.4. Schematic representation of "logistization"
category content relating to cultural services

The logistics final stage and its highest form is the creation of able-to-work logistic systems. The latter represent a system of structure management in the sphere of commonweal activities allowing to settle timely the whole group of interrelated tactical and strategic tasks which ensure the optimization of integrated flow processes taking place in these structures according to specified criteria (incomes, profit, costs, service quality, competitiveness and others).

As it seems, the logistization category should be defined with account of management trend, goals, sources and objects. In addition, considering that the logistization process might be being directed towards economic systems of different levels, in our opinion, the interpretation of this concept may take this aspect into account also. A schematic representation of given category is shown on Fig. 4.4.

Therefore, the author approaches the definition of logistization from a broad scope consideration. It appears necessary to divide all of the services into homogeneous groups, subgroups, kinds and varieties according to sufficiently large number of independent and mutually connected classificational features to facilitate the process of these all services analysis and management and also of perfection of their record.

In this regard, the author's definition of this category is proposed. The process of creative industry logistization, in our opinion, should be considered at finale as a process of systematic, long-term, targeted end-to-end management of resource flows in order to provide for needed service availability in required quantity and of set quality in the right place at the right time for particular consumer with the lowest cost being done through the socio-cultural sphere. The logistization process is carried out in accordance with logistic principles, strategic goals on the basis of resources reproduction, developed standards of social-cultural services introduction, assumes the development of life quality of creative services consumers. Based on the aforesaid, the logistization process embraces main characteristics of innovation process.

However, logistization's main core and goal is the provision of necessary rationality (optimality) of flow processes management and fulfillment, thereby, of additional reserves through the implementation of more successful variants of productive forces interaction. Pointed reserves' value depends on demands' implementation by management systems which accordingly, managing and managed systems must be adequate by their complexity and structural diversity to the management object.

The effect of this operation pursuing will far exceed an additional benefit of market structures from management optimal organization of their flow processes. Existing features of socio-cultural service management systems dictate necessity to embody multi-stage logistization of given systems in the form of formation of macro- and micro-logistic systems of socio-cultural service.

Macro-logistics provides for logistization high level when management organization covers activities, control and service of several participants in providing of socio-cultural services connected with each other by mutually beneficial program. As a result, a single logistic chain is being formed for several economic entities not only in the provision of socio-cultural services but also those in marketing, financial, information, market activities etc.

Micro-logistics provides a rational organization of work in intra-company processes, mainly aimed at the increasing of job efficiency of the organizations themselves, at the service quality improving and provided services cost reduction.

The pointed approach makes it possible to build management systems of socio-cultural services adapted to changing needs of clients, forming effective management of passenger traffic and of client flows, information services, insurance, organization pricing policy [4, p. 41]. At finale, the necessity occurs on changing of relation information model between agents and counterparties. The involving of socio- cultural service organizations into market economy requires the creation of new organizational-economic forms of logistic processes with information technologies obligatory introduction.

The actuality of creating a management logistic system for socio-cultural services rises due to that the services system is underdeveloped in Russia economy, the needed and sufficient conditions to provide for required performance of formed management logistic systems of socio-cultural services lack.

The logistization mechanism of creative services system is being realized as a regular, purposeful process of influence, at all levels and all stages of services formation and movement, on the factors and conditions ensuring achievement and maintenance of economical and effective process of functioning of the socio-cultural services and welfare system in the market. Organizational efforts, targeted the logistization efficiency rise, can be consolidated into two aspects: operational and strategic.

In Western countries, the creative services sphere is considered as one of the important sectors of economy to invest. According to UNCTAD statistical data, the growth rate of international trade in the creative services was 3% in 2016, larger increment (4.5%) was observed only in the trade of computer and information services. All this testifies to the growing importance of contribution of the creative industry to economic development in modern conditions and to the prospects of this industry development.

Comparing culture sphere financing in Russia in the context of international oppositions, Russia closes the list of 25 countries by consumption per capita on culture, just leaving Greece and Bulgaria behind.

Further global integration of society, culture and business requires new mechanisms to provide for the creative industry development in Russia with account of development world experience, maximization of resource potential usage and adoption of management verified organizational-economic mechanisms for the development of the culture industry.

Currently, the underdevelopment of organizational-economic forms and insufficient elaboration of mechanisms for support and strategic development of the creative industry hampers this sphere evolution, and the structure of investment sources of RF socio-cultural projects reveals a disproportion between public and private sectors and asymmetry between needs and opportunities for pointed projects financing.

The formation of logistization optimal mode of the creative industry with its subsequent adjustment in accordance with structural and market changes is the content of operational organizational work. Together, the essence of logistization process management is mainly defined by sectoral priorities in region, i.e. that is specific in terms of implementation ways and methods. In its turn, the creation of favorable conditions for capital investment into region economy infrastructure sector, as a material base of socio-cultural service sphere, is a strategic organizational direction of general character.

REFERENCE LIST

1. National accounts 2018 // Federal State Statistics Service-URL: http://www.gks.ru/wps/wcm/connect/rosstat_main/rosstat/ru/statistics/accounts/# (accessed 12.05.2019) *(in Russian)*.
2. Office for National Statistics. URL: https://www.gov.uk (accessed 12.05.2019) *(in Russian)*.
3. Protsenko I.O. Innovative Logistics — Prospects and Realities // Journal of Russian Entrepreneurship. — 2005. — No. 12 (72). — pp. 89–94. — URL: http://www.creativeconomy.ru/articles/7294/ (accessed 12.05.2019) *(in Russian)*.
4. Malshina N.A. Methodology of Flow Processes Interaction in Logistic Chains of Socio-cultural Service Sysytem // Izvestiya Saratov University. New series. Series: Economics. Management.Right. 2013. T. 13. — No. 1-1. — pp. 38–42.*(in Russian)*.

5. OPPORTUNITIES OF EFFICIENCY INCREASE OF FLOW PROCESSES IN LOGISTICS SYSTEMS ON THE BASIS OF TRADITIONAL CONCEPTS: MATERIAL, INFORMATION, FINANCIAL AND LABOR FLOWS

Logistics in the modern conditions finds broad development not only in the manufacturing industry but also in the service sphere. Recent years, logistics methods find application in tourism industry. It seems necessary to consider general principles of logistics, its concepts and directions which are typical for the tourist activities.

The logistics system of the tourist enterprise includes the following components:

1. Information — tour planning, order processing, demand forecasting.
2. Tourists transportation — choice of transport kind and carrier company.
3. Tourist serving personnel — is an important component of the logistics system. Much importance is referred to their selection and training.
4. Serving production — is logistics units that serve tour forming and consumer services provision.

Production capacities and economic adaptability of the tourist enterprise have important role for logistics system functioning. Its important problem is to determine tourist enterprise size. Thus, the processes of formation, promotion and implementation of the tourist product as well as their related financial and information flows have been becoming the objects of logistics management and control in tourism.

The subject of tourism logistics is a theory and a practical activity of planning, organization, functional management and control of motion processes of human, financial, labor, legal and information flow set in the tourism activities sphere.

Principles of forming of logistics activities content in a tourism organization are: consistency (a selection of objects as separately managed sub-system and an application towards sub-system of system approach); complexity (content formation on the basis of recording of all types of tour-business provision); scientific character (recording of calculation origin on all stages of flow management); specificity (content formation on the basis of clear definition of particular result as a goal of flow motion); constructiveness (permanent adjustment of variable part of training course content); reliability (content constant part forming); efficiency (determination on achievement of minimum of logistic expenses); flexibility (embeddedness of trend prognosis ability into logistic system); integrity (provides content assessment of logistic course as a single whole).

Application of logistics main principles, using regional market environment and system of logistic communications in the conditions of real assembly of material, transport, financial, monetary, labor, information and other flows, which interaction between objects of tourism sphere proceed through, allows to increase significantly the efficiency of their functioning.

Originating from the conceptual statements of logistics, the main functions of logistics in the tourism are:

1) operational analysis, control and management of the processes of formation, promotion and implementation of the tourist product as well as of strategic planning and forecasting of the activities of the tourist organizations;
2) operational transmission (acquiring) of a necessary volume and quality of information at a given time and into a right place;
3) operational control over motion (transfer) of tourists and a tourist product;
4) integration of separately functioning information systems of touristic infrastructure (local networks, regional networks, transcontinental networks, etc.) into a single logistic information system;
5) calculation and organization of a financial buffer in the case of economic force majeure occurrence on the basis of analysis and forecasting of negative trends in the tourism sphere;
6) provision of holding of conference calls, video conferences, symposiums etc. of employees and tourist organization representatives on a local, regional and global level.

Material, financial, information and service flows traditionally constitute the objects of logistic research as a science and a logistics management as an entrepreneurship sphere.

There are several definitions of a material flow considering various aspects of its functioning. However, all of them have similar points in understanding a semantic component of this concept, which as a result of main characteristics are revealed: a composition of material flow includes various material resources, an integral function of motion, an application to these resources of logistic operations and functions. In the modern logistics, the concept of a material flow is defined as products, considered in applying to them of various logistic operations and referred to a time interval. If products are not in a motion state, they go into a backlog. Thus, the material flow in time certain moments can be a backlog of material resources, unfinished production or ready products.

Material flow is characterized by a certain set of parameters and can be classified according to different features. Parameters of material flows can be: nomenclature, range and products quantity; dimensional characteristics (volume, area, linear sizes); weight characteristics (total weight, gross weight, net weight); physical-chemical characteristics of the cargo; characteristics of tare (packaging), carrier, vehicle (load capacity, cargo capacity); terms of sale contract (transfer of ownership, delivery); conditions of transportation and insurance; financial (cost) characteristics; conditions for performing other physical distribution operations associated with products transfer, etc. Material flow can be characterized by such indicators as intensity, density, speed, starting and ending points, path trajectory, path length, etc.

There are other features of classification being distinguished besides shown in the figure– in relation to logistic system; in relation to logistic system link; in relation to logistic system subsystem; according to physical-chemical properties; according to cargo specific weight; according to flow element transmission character; according to degree of flow elements grading; according to intensity; according to compatibility. The dimension of the material flow is the ratio of measurement unit to time unit.

Under traditional approach, the tasks on material flow management in each link (production, transportation, sales, etc.) were solved to a large extent separately. Individual links were presented as closed systems, isolated from other subsystems. Use of logistic method for material flow management is characterized by the following features: single body is created ensuring optimal use of total material flow; technological processes are adjusted in accordance with the requirements to optimize total material flow; optimal delivery schemes and schedules are developed; order sizes, frequency, types of deliveries, etc. are determined; deliveries methods and kinds are optimized and made specialized that meet the requirements of namely total material flow.

The use of logistics method is characterized by a systematic approach to the formation of logistic system that provides optimization of the total material flow, allowing to:
- rise the use degree of material and technical base;
- optimize the inventory of all participants of logistic process;
- provide the delivery of necessary good (service) of necessary quality to a necessary place, at given time with the least expenses;
- increase the range, quality and level of logistic service and office.

The above logistics principles are generally accepted and provide an opportunity to study flows and apply an adequate control mechanism, but other features can be included into the classifications at necessity and depending on the situation.

The material flow in tourism is understood as translocations (transitions, trips) of RF citizens, foreign citizens from a permanent place of residence for recreational, educational, professional, sportive and other purposes without engaging in paid activities to a country (place) of temporary stay and back, as well as the flow of residents applying to travel agencies for tourist vouchers, to air, railway, sea, river ticket offices for the purchase of travel tickets; to embassies and VRDs (Visa and Registration Department) for obtaining exit, entry visas, etc.

Each material flow corresponds to some information flow. Information flow — the flow of messages in oral, documentary (paper and electronic) and other forms, accompanying the material or service flow in considered logistic system and intended mainly for the implementation of managing functions. It is possible to distinguish elementary, key and supporting information flows accompanying corresponding operations and functions. As well as, different approaches to definition of indicators of information flows are emphasized.

Many scientists and researchers agree that the dominant role belongs to information circulating in logistic systems in the managing and controlling material, financial, service, labor flows. The use of logistic method to ensure the optimization of information flow will allow to:
- increase degree and quality of use of material-technical base;
- optimize inventory of all participants of logistic process;
- provide delivery of necessary goods (services) of a necessary quality to a necessary place, at set time with the least expenses;
- increase range, quality and level of logistic services;
- optimize delivery process to end-consumer;
- align quality of expected and actual product presented;
- organize operational information exchange between suppliers and consumers;
- provide possibility of independent participation of a consumer in end-product formation.

Information flows are interrelated directly and form financial flows of logistic system. In market economy conditions, efficiency rise of usage of information, material flows is achieved mainly by improvement of their financial services that is possible only under condition of logistic methods and principles application.

Financial flows in the form of motion (translocation) of monetary, currency and securities have always existed while organizing and conducting economic and entrepreneurial activities. It seems possible to define financial flows as directed motion of financial resources associated with material, information and other flows both within logistic system frames and outside it. Financial flows arise from the reimbursement of logistic costs and expenditures, the fund raise from financing sources, the reimbursement (in monetary terms) for products sold and services rendered to participants of logistic chain. Financial flows are heterogeneous in composition, motion directions, target and a number of other features. The need in identification of the most effective ways to manage financial flows in logistics necessitates to pursue their detailed classification.

With introduction of logistic methods of material flow management and control to industrial and economic activity of state and economic entities, the traditional essence of financial flows has undergone substantial changes, which main one is following:

- logistic financial flow (LFF) — is not just financial resources motion but is their directional motion;
- LFF means funds motion — only in logistic systems or between them;
- LFF specifics — is the need to serve the process of moving in space and time of corresponding material flow.

Financial service mechanism of material flows in tourist activities is currently the least studied area of the logistics: some issues are omitted completely from the consideration in specialized literature; as to other part of issues, essential discrepancies in understanding of financial flow essence itself are seen. It seems possible at its part to look into currently existing problematic in this work frames.

The interrelation of material and financial flows is realized via tourist market which represents the sphere of economic relations between producers and consumers of tourism product. The tourist market is characterized by the presence of legal entities and individuals who are the producers and consumers of tourism products. The functioning of the tourist market can be demonstrated as follows (Fig. 5.1):

1. A tourist (consumer) pays to a tourist organization (travel agent or tour operator) the money for package tour.
2. A tourism organization gives package tour to a tourist.
3. A tourist embodies package tour for a tourist product.
4. A tourist embodies a tourist product.
5. A tourist organization invests monetary funds into development of tourist market, tourist industry and creation of tourist services new types.
6. A tourist organization forms new types of a tourist product.
7. A tourist organization pays taxes to the budget.

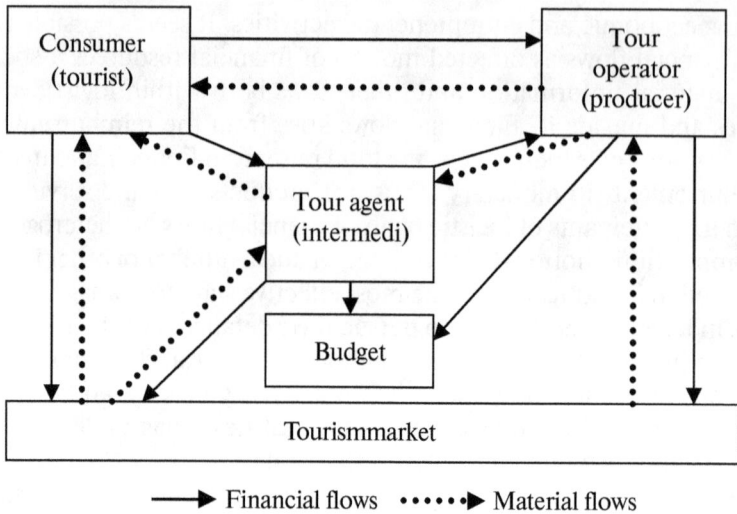

Figure 5.1. Scheme of material and financial flows of tourism market.

The main purpose of financial service of material flows in logistics is to provide their motion by financial resources in necessary volumes, in needed time frames and with utilization of the most effective financing sources. The variety of forms and directions of modern financial market development as well as specifics of its functioning determines wide use of securities and financial instruments derivatives during financial service of material flows.

The following functions are marked as fundamental ones of tourism market:

1. implementation of value and user value implied in a tourist product;
2. organization of the process of bringing a tourist product to a tourist;
3. investment of funds into tourism industry development and formation of new types of tourism product.

Also, in various scientific sources, there is a distinguishing of service flows into a logistic system separate component which is referred to services flows (of intangible activities, special type of products or good) generated by logistics system as a whole or its subsystem (link, element) in order to satisfy external or internal consumers of business organization.

The term "service", accepted in the international standard ISO 8402:1994, means the results of immediate interaction between supplier and consumer and supplier internal activities to meet consumer needs. Service is understood as — the process of providing a service — supplier activity that is necessary for service provision. Despite the service importance, effective ways of its quality assessment are still absent that is explained by series of service specificities in comparison with products' characteristics. Such specificities (service flow characteristics) are:

1. Intangibility of service. It means difficulty for service providers to explain and specify service as well as difficulties to evaluate it on the part of a buyer.
2. Buyer often takes immediate part in the production of services.
3. Services are consumed at the time of their production, i.e. services are not stored or transported.
4. Buyer never becomes service owner.
5. Service — is an activity (process) and therefore cannot be tested until buyer buys it.
6. Service often consists of a system of smaller (sub-service) services, moreover, buyer evaluates these sub-services.

Consideration of integrated logistic system service flows seems more effective to investigate in connection with traditionally existing flow processes as well as innovative ones but which have proved their scientific justification -the labor flows. Within this approach framework, the dynamics of logistic system all elements at the input, during processing and at the output as well as production entire infrastructure functioning are more objectively reflected. Service flows can be seen as a result of target integration of material, information, financial and labor flows in dependence of type and form of rendered services in the process of their bringing to a consumer and immediate realization in various quantities and various combinations.

Providing services implies mandatory immediate customer participation; at the moment of meeting of an integrated flow and a custom, the process of service provision takes place. Different types of flows in different theories take priority depending on the aspects of logistic system functioning, The composition of service system integrated flow is in constant dynamics and depends on provided services kind (Fig. 5.2).

Considered mechanism plays a significant role in total logistic process, forming a significant part of logistic flows both inside and outside of organization.

It is possible to define labor flows as — groups of economically active population in the process of application to them of operations on formation, transformation, translocation and realization of labor potential which they can act in as either a subject or an object of economic relations, pursuing translocation in geographical, structural-hierarchical, information-experimental spaces and referred to a time period. This type of flow processes is rather detailed presented in a whole series of

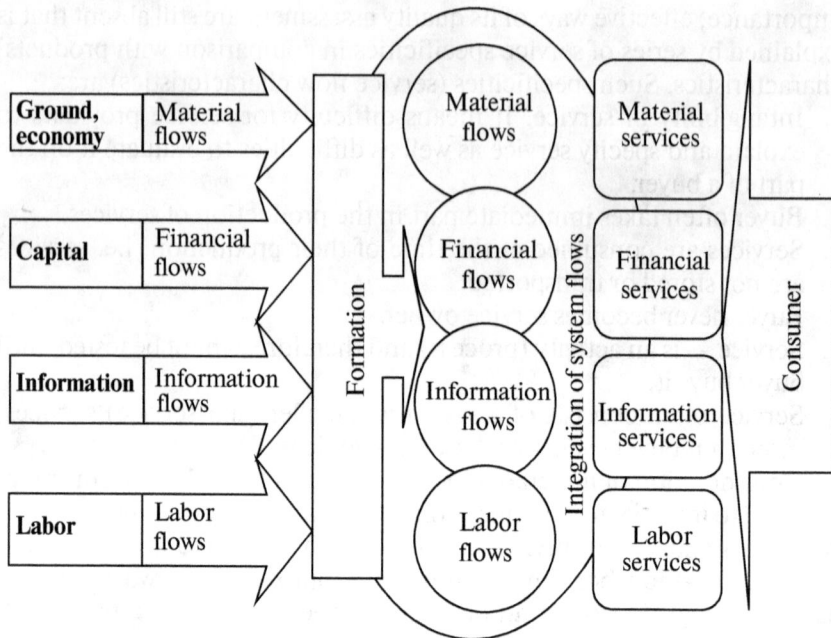

Figure 5.2. Formation of logistic flows during the services providing

scientific studies that premised on there is no need to consider longer the logistic system within this stage discussion.

The quality and attractiveness of the service depend on the ability of a consumer to evaluate the service at finale (to evaluate in general). The pointed characteristics and features of service flows play an important role in the logistic process, particularly, in the field of goods distribution. It is important to take into account the fact that service quality in the logistics is manifested at the moment when a service provider and a consumer meet in a personal contact.

It looks possible to formulate the following conclusion based on the pursued analysis of flow processes, on the basis of traditional approach — introduction and usage of logistic technologies in tourism activities will allow to:

• create a unified system of record and control over formation and motion of tourist product;
• cut time parameters of material, financial and information flows promotion;
• automate processes of record and control of material, financial and information flows;

- cut time interval and improve service quality of tourist product consumers;
- cut number of staff, reduce volume of circulating documentation, reduce significantly number of errors and failures in record-report documentation, etc.

The beginning of 1990s is characterized by a reorientation of production sector into service sector. Entrepreneurs began to pay more attention not only to product itself but also to service quality: timely delivery at right time and to right place. There was a work improvement in the service sector without requirement of additional capital investments for new goods production, nevertheless, being able to ensure manufacturer high competitiveness by transport costs reduction, supplies reliability improvement, intermediaries number reduction, funds turnover increase, etc.

It is fair to give the following definition of logistics in tourism taking into account the legislative and other regulatory-legal acts providing tourism activities: logistics in tourism — is a science about system planning, forecasting, management and control of process of formation, promotion and realization of tourist product in accordance with interests and requirements of potential consumers (tourists) as well as about off-the-cuff and reliable exchange of messages in human-machine information systems with the lowest financial costs. In 1985, Board of Logistic Management clarified then-existing definition of logistics in the following way: "Logistics is the process of planning, management and control of efficient (from the view of costs cut) flow of inventories of raw products, materials, goods in process, finished products, services and related information from the origin of this flow to the place of consumption (including import, export, internal and external motions) for the purposes of full satisfaction of consumers' needs". The following points are essential in this definition:
- logistic activities have an integrated character and extend from the point of origin to the point of consumption of material resources and finished products flow;
- importance of related information management is stressed;
- intangible (service) flows of services are included into the logistics sphere. This has a fundamental significance for the development of logistic approaches to the service industry (tourism industry), because previously, the object of study and optimization in the logistics were only material flows.

Broadly, logistics is science about management and optimization of material flows, service flows and related information and financial flows in particular micro-, meso- or macroeconomic system for to achieve objectives put in front of it.

Narrowly (from business perspective), logistics — is an integrated management tool enabling achievement of strategic, tactical or operational goals of business enterprises by means of effective (total costs reduction and meeting the needs of end-consumers on quality of products and services) management of material and service flows as well as of referred to them flows of information and financial resources.

The ability of logistic systems to adaption to external environment conditions is caused by the uncertainty of environment and its development. In these conditions, the ability of logistic systems to adapt to external environment changes is an essential factor of financial stability in sales market of goods and services.

Logistics concept in tourism is, first of all, in the change of detached activities of participants of formation, promotion and implementation of tourist product in favor of systemic (integrated) activities. The concept essence is in — reduction of costs (expenses) on people (tourists) moving (transportation) from the permanent place of residence to the place (country) of temporary stay as well as on tourist product promotion from its seller (supplier — tour operator, travel agent) to end consumer (tourist). Uniqueness of logistic concept is in integration of all individual functions into a single whole with the purpose of minimization of total costs to the required level of service of a customer.

The possibility to consider economic resources in the form of flow processes as well as the application feasibility of logistic approach specifics to these types of resources of services sector are fragmentary seen in studies of Russian and foreign authors. Together, processes of management and dynamics of resources of recreational sector, services sector are viewed at both, micro- and macro- levels of systems. Regarding material, information and financial resources, statements of the system approach and integrated resource management are colligated in a specific of logistic approach; the specific is in distinguishing a single function of management of previously disparate elements of the process of resource formation, translocation, transformation and takeover. Theory and practice of foreign companies functioning prove effectiveness of this approach application in resource management. Usage of basic statements of logistic approach as well as of individual logistic principles for management efficiency improvement of economic resources will allow to ensure the possibility of increase of logistic system stability of service and tourism sphere by the way of their closer interaction through integration both in the logistic chain itself and with the dynamical external environment. The integrated approach makes it possible to combine logistic functional areas by coordination of actions performed by independent links of logistic system sharing common responsibility in target function frames.

In accordance with main functional areas of logistics in the field of tourist service and other services provision, the main practical tasks which face decision adoptions are:

- perfection of the process of formation, promotion and implementation of service product;
- perfection of the process of delivery and transportation of consumers and producers, service providers;
- perfection of the process of organization of operational information exchange between suppliers and consumers of service product;
- perfection of the process of organization, planning, forecasting and control of logistic flow processes.

Essence of the integral paradigm is in that in the process of orders fulfillment, the service system elements are considered as a single whole. Labor and service flow processes are added to the traditional types of logistics flows — material, financial and information, at the present stage of logistics development. Now it is possible to speak with confidence about formed second direction of logistic science — service logistics which substance is in study of managing of human and other kinds of flow processes, performing role to serve towards traditionally outlined flow processes. There are two main types of service logistics: entrepreneurial service logistics or macro-level of service logistics which studies so-called primary service flows or service flows with independent demand; service logistics as an integral part of resource motion logistics which necessity in usage arises from the obligations of trading/industrial enterprise to consumers, who purchased machinery and equipment from particular enterprise; it means that this kind of service logistics studies secondary service flows or service flows with dependent demand. Based on this, the entrepreneurial service logistics is understood as logistics branch devoted to design, forming and optimization of service concentration-distribution systems and their effective use in the management of service flows in the internal and external environment of trading/industrial enterprise. We will call service logistics as the branch of resource motion logistics devoted to management of service flows in micro- and macro- logistical systems. Service flows of service sector are understood as flows of intangible activities generated by logistics system in a whole or its subsystem provided to a customer with the purpose to meet his needs. Relatively the types of service logistics, the definition of service flows makes it possible to talk about the presence of these flow processes in each from the proposed kinds of service logistics, however, these flow processes are different by the orientation and the functioning process. In the frames of service logistics first kind, the service flows are directed to a range of services, in the frames of service logistics second kind — to a customer service process. It seems possible to speak about distinguishing of service flow processes into a separate object of logistics research regardless of the proposed modern kinds of service logistics.

Need for participation of labor flows in the process of providing services does not cause any questions since the very specificity of services implies necessarily immediate participation of service manufacturer and service consumer. Use of logistic concept statements to improve the efficiency of human resources management has been researched in the works of such authors as B. Anikin, D. Bauersox, A. Gadzhinsky, M. Gordon, L. Mirotin, O. Novikov, B. Plotnikov, A. Semenenko, V. Sergeev, A. Smekhov, S. Uvarov, A. Fomenko, V. Shcherbakov.

Within the listed flow processes, it is reflected the translocation of all dynamic elements of logistic system at input, during processing and at output, as well as it is reflected the functioning of entire infrastructure of production of both, goods and services. It is viewed possible to look on service flows as a result of targeted integration of the above-listed types of logistics flows. Depending on the type and form of services rendered during their bringing to consumer and direct implementation in various combinations and quantities, material, information, financial and labor flows are involved. The process of services provision can be considered as a process of specific production which input resources and their transformation are in accordance with the interests and requirements of immediate consumers.

The concept of service as a service of population in various spheres of everyday life includes all traditionally underlined types of logistic flows — material, financial, information, labor ones, as if combining them as a result of the activity — service. Another necessary component of the logistic system of services is a consumer because service necessarily requires his immediate presence. Schematically, it is possible to present this system in the form of interrelated flow processes showing in any elements of logistic system; it seems major and prior to identify non-material, non-tangible flows — information flows and service flows.

Integration of material, financial, information and labor flows forms the base of service system, which, transforming them, forms integrated flows of orientation and specificity accordingly services provided types. At the stage of services direct provision implying the moment of meeting between a consumer and a producer, a collision of integral flow in the form of ready-on service and consumer takes place.

The process of providing services involves mandatory direct participation of a consumer, at the moment of meeting of integrated flow and consumer, the process of providing services takes place. Depending on the aspects of logistic system functioning, different types of flows take priority. The composition of integrated flow of service system is in constant dynamics and depends on services provided type.

Quality and attractiveness of service depends on the ability of a consumer to evaluate it at the end (in general). Characteristics and features of service flows play an important role in logistic process. It is very important to take into account the fact that service quality in logistics is manifested at the moment when a service provider and a consumer meet personally.

The integrated paradigm provides an opportunity to increase the stability of logistic systems by ensuring their closer interaction that requires further integration both in logistics chain itself and with dynamic external environment. At the same time, to solve these tasks the traditional paradigm is not enough as a rule. Therefore, in the current conditions, the integral paradigm of logistics becomes particularly relevant providing a synthesis of elements of logistic system integrated on the basis of material, labor and other logistics flow that implies a new scheme of interaction.

REFERENCE LIST

1. Sergeev V.I. Management in Business Logistics // M.: INF. ed. House "FILIN", 1997.
2. Innovation Resources: Organizational, Financial, Administrative: Studies. no. // Edited by Prof. — M. UNITY-DANA, 2003.
3. Effectiveness of Logistics Management: Textbook for High Schools // Under editorship of L.B. Mirotin. M.: Publishing house "Examination", 2004. — 448 pp.
4. Malshina N.A. Organizational and Economic Mechanism of Logistics of Social and Cultural Service Providing Innovative Development of the Volga Region. //Innovative Bulletin of Regions. No. 1. 2013. — 5–11 pp.
5. Plotnikov A.N., Pchelintseva I.N. Management of Social Investment of Microeconomic Systems: Monograph // Saratov. 2009. — 173 p.

6. SPECIFICITY OF RESOURCE FLOW PROCESSES IN SERVICE SPHERE

The specificity of flow processes of service sector and tourist services, in particular, is defined by the characteristic signs which are present in different types of flows of a given system. Thus, material flows mainly constitute commodity-intangible values: formation, promotion and implementation of a tourist product and its constituent intangible services. The material flows in a tourism are understood as "moving (transitions, travel) of citizens of the Russian Federation, foreign citizens and stateless persons from their permanent place of residence for health, educational, professional-business, sports, religious and other purposes without engaging in paid activities in the country (place) of temporary stay as well as understood as flow of citizens applying to travel agencies for tourist vouchers, into air, railway, sea, river ticket offices for the purchase of travel tickets; into embassies and DVRs (Departments of Visas and Registration) for obtaining exit, entry visas, etc." []. Financial flows of tourism services in the framework of being fulfilled operations provide for not individual one-time payments but for a lot of time-distributed monetary receipts (payments) and pays. It seems possible to define financial flows as directed motion of financial resources associated with material, information and other types of flows both within a logistics system and outside it. An information flow can be defined as information being considered in the process of its motion in space and time in a certain direction. A typical example of the distribution of information flows in the tourism industry is the functioning of human-machine computer systems on line and off line. The specificity of information flows in the sphere of tourist services is in the need to combine a lot of information at one time, in one place, with proper quality and with account of consumer requirements.

Based on pursued analysis of flow processes of services sphere, it seems possible to assert — the introduction and use of logistics principles in the tourism activities will allow to:
- create a unified system of record and control over formation and motion of a tourist product;
- reduce time parameters of material, financial and information flows promotion;
- automate processes of record and control of material, financial and information, labor flows;

- reduce time interval and improve quality of service of tourist product consumers;
- reduce number of serving staff, reduce volume of circulating documentation, significantly reduce number of errors and failures in record-report documentation, etc.

Prerequisites are being created for the construction of a logistics management system of an organization on the basis of a systematic approach on the level of different types of resource flows in service enterprises. This logistic management system is a structured adaptive system consisting of elements connected by service, financial and information, labor flows. Creation and consideration of the logistic management system of a service enterprise is aimed at optimizing the use of resources, increasing the efficiency of activities, improving the quality of service. Based on the definition of information, financial, labor and service flows, the organizational structure of the logistics system is built in an enterprise. Flow management pursued on the information remains a little-studied area of the service business.

The logistics process for the formation and promotion of a tourist product includes following stages: research; experiment; development of technological documentation and personnel training for the formation and promotion of tourist products; organization and pursuing of advertising.

At the first stage, research is carried out on the development of new tours, types of services and goods. From 5 to 15% of funds, assigned for whole process, are expended on this job. The scope of research includes tour concepts and programs, the potential demand for a tourist product, etc. is specified; environmental and price working out of the issue (development of a business plan, its economic justification, etc.) is held.

The subjects of logistics research in the tourism sector can also be:
- volume, structure and dynamics of production and consumption of a tourist product: what firms operate and where; what services are offered and how it relates to international standards; which market segments are involved; socio-economic and socio-demographic data of consumer groups; what routes and how many days are offered, etc.;
- availability and level of reserves: what are the reserves of a tourist organization to increase the coverage of consumers (tourists), to expand the geography of routes, range of services, service program options, etc.,
- price motion: what is the price level for similar services of competing firms, what is the average market rate of prices for certain services, etc.,

- market participants (partners, competitors, suppliers of products, intermediaries, consumers of services, etc.);
- manner of research, production-sales, advertising and other activities in the market for the implementation of a tourist product.

That is why Russian tourist organizations should introduce modern logistics systems of goods distribution sticking to positive foreign experience.

Specificity of logistics principles application in the field of tourism is manifested in the endowing logistics fundamental definitions with the specific aspects — so material flows mainly constitute commodity-intangible values: the formation, promotion and implementation of a tourist product and its constituent intangible services.

Material flows in the tourism are understood as translocations (transitions, travel) of citizens of the Russian Federation, foreign citizens and stateless persons from their permanent place of residence for health, educational, professional, business, sports, religious and other purposes without engaging in paid activities with the country (place) of temporary stay as well as understood as flow of citizens applying to travel agencies for tourist vouchers, to air-, railway-, sea-, river-ticket offices for purchase of travel tickets; to embassies and DVRs to obtain exit, entry visas, etc. Such an extensive definition, according to the author's opinion, has a number of drawbacks — blurred boundaries, inaccuracy, extensive scope of the definition which requires mandatory revision and clarification. With the traditional approach to material flows management in each link of system, the tasks were being solved separately, isolated from partners' systems technically, economically, technologically and methodologically by means of planning and administration methods. The application of the logistic approach to the management of material flows is characterized by the following features:

1. logistic process participants create a single body having purpose to optimize the total material flow;
2. technological processes in links (production, sales, transportation and others) are adjusted in accordance with the requirements of optimal organization of total material flow;
3. orders' schemes are designed or modeled, optimal size, frequency and types, order batching, shipping methods, etc are determined;
4. optimal routes and schedules for tourist product purchase are being developed;
5. transport park of necessary vehicles, allowing to optimize total material flow, is being developed.

Formation of an integrated tourist product

LOGISTICS: analysis, evaluation, management (regulation), control

Transportation of tourists (consumers)

Promotion of tourist product

Planning, forecasting and control of financial flows

Organization and implementation of information

Realization (selling) of tourist product

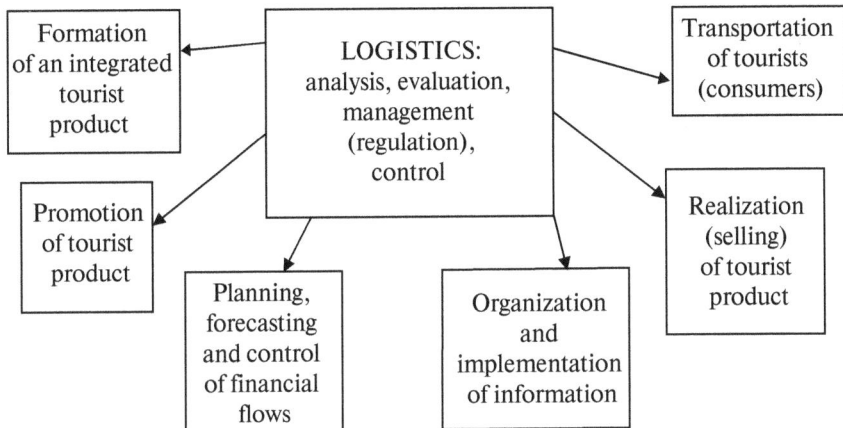

Figure 6.1. Directions of application of logistic principles in the system of tourist service

The analysis of characteristic features of logistic approach application to material flow management shows that all participants of logistic process have common purpose of formation of such logistic system which would provide rational organization of total material flow that is reached with the use of system approach to formation of logistic system. The application of a systematic approach to material flow management in the process of logistic system forming will allow to:

1. increase usage degree of material-technical base of formation and realization of a tourist product;
2. optimize commodity (food) and other stocks of logistic process all participants;
3. provide delivery of necessary goods (product) of necessary quality to necessary place at set time with the least expenses;
4. increase range, quality and level of services and logistic service.

Financial flows in the frames of being fulfilled operations represent not individual one-time payments but a set of time-distributed cash receipts (payments) and pays-off. Financial flows in tourism sector can be divided into the following groups:

1. financial flows for the sale of tourist products;
2. financial flows of the cash flow of the firm;
3. investment financial flows;
4. financial flows between:
   a) founders, shareholders and tour organization (domestic significance);
   b) travel agency and state (budgetary and extra-budgetary fords);

c) travel agency and contractors, subcontractors;
d) travel agency and insurance company;
e) travel agency and credit-banking institutions;
f) travel agency and its employees.

A typical example of information flow distribution in the tourism industry is the functioning of human-machine computer systems on line and off line. Computer system on line allows to exchange information in "dialogue" mode: travel company representative has an opportunity to exchange information with service providers and potential consumers. System off line is applicable as an e-mail exchange with the help of specialized programs of two types: servers supported by companies, network providers, and e-mail clients.

Followed from the above, application of the logistic principles in the field of information flow management is of particular importance in the field of services. It is the service sector, having its main characteristic as complexity, is aimed at the combination of several flows of services in a certain time period that requires the adoption of operational high-efficiency decisions. For to achieve those, the use of information technologies sounds like the best option. This is the area where the service sphere business can gain advantages and a spot for future competition.

Interrelation of financial and related information flows in the relations of subjects of the tourism sector is possible to consider in the form of a logistic scheme.

The most significant features of financial flows of tourist companies in various organizational-legal forms include: authorized capital formation, obtained profit distribution, relationships with budget. It should also be noted that the specifics of financial flows of tourism services include:

- form of rendered services obtaining — with a tour operator on tourist reception (meet-company) or without a tour operator on tourist reception;
- implementation method of formed tour package — directly to tourists or travel agents;
- tour operator (or travel agent) can provide tourists with additional individual services: insurance, providing with visas and passports, obtaining of air tickets, etc.

Depending on this or that scheme, the schemes of cash payments for rendered services and the amount of taxation change that affects a logistic system in a whole and a financial flow scheme.

Legal entities (commercial and non-commercial organizations) as well as individuals from the moment of their registration as an individual entrepreneur have the right to carry out tourist activities. Forming and using of various funds have its aim to provide for economic activity of a travel company with necessary funds. Monetary funds of a travel company are divided into two groups:

- equity funds, including authorized capital, reserve fund, accumulation and special purpose funds, retained earnings;
- funds of attracted and borrowed monetary resources consisting of: long-term and short-term bank credits, loans, securities, etc.

Monetary funds of a travel company — are a source (resource) of organization's asset formation. Effectiveness of business activities of tourism organization largely depends on the ratio of non-current and current assets of a company, the assets are the subject to general golden rules of financing. Optimization of assets and related resources of monetary funds especially requires the account of regularities of external environment which causes great impact on financial performance indicators of a travel company that doesn't appear possible to solve without the involvement of logistic principles and methods of management, planning and forecasting of financial flows within logistic systems, between them, between logistic systems and the environment. Seems possible to define a logistic financial flow in tourism as — a purposeful motion of funds and securities within logistic system or between logistic systems and external environment in order to maximize the accumulated financial fund and minimize costs.

Features of labor flows dynamics in socio-cultural services and tourism sphere are manifested in a high percentage show of staff turnover. Specificity of market of a tourist, hotel and service personnel in a whole is a staff high turnover which is about 30% according to some estimates. Hotel companies lack both top-management staff as top-managers and employees of lower positions — as maids, waiters. A large number of young professionals leave the hotel business after the first year of work. At the level of top management, this process is explained by the lack of specialists, newly opened hotels have to lure managers from existing ones, creating certain preferential working conditions. In low positions, the migration is associated with low wages, high loads and stresses.

The specificity of labor potential of hotel and restaurant service is also the multiplicity of necessary personnel for full value functioning. The higher the class of the hotel, the more staff it needs. There are three employees per guest in average in an upper-class hotel, this ratio is about one to one in middle-class hotels. The staff of the four-star hotel with 185 rooms are 195 employees. With the increase in the number of hotel enterprises projected according to the World Tourism and Travel Council (WTTC), the number of employees in the hotel industry may increase on another 50%.

Also, the specifics of the labor resources of the socio-cultural services sector is, as a rule, small formats of enterprises, large corporations in this type of business, according to various estimates, occupy in percentage no more than 40%. The staff of small organizations demands qualified management. The main difference of staff work in small enterprises of the service sector is in that employees do not have a clearly delineated sphere of authority. The employee often performs several functions and must quickly settle the arising business issues. Regulation of staff quantity required in small organizations in most cases assumes combining of functional responsibilities of some staff categories. Personnel work standardization comes out on first place to increase work speed and quality in large organizations of the service sector but individual approach to each consumer is necessary in small forms of business organization. Personal contact with a visitor allows to make him feel not as a client, but as a guest. Skillful combination by personnel of several functions is considered as organization's competitive advantage. Skilful distribution of labor resources, the concentration of labor flows at activity certain nodes within service small organizations are an essential condition of service enterprise managing.

Following the importance of personal qualities and skills of service personnel, the matter of training of organization staff potential occurs. The beginning of labor flow formation goes on in educational institutions. In Russia, in contrast to Europe, the system of educational institutions, which train specialists in the field of services, is just starting its establishment and development, and service enterprises, including hotels, are forced to do it on their own. The labor flows can pass through a different number of different types of educational institutions, which upon completion of, through the primary labor market, must convey the formed labor potential in the form of knowledge and skills to a consumer in the form of an organization-employer. Consistent motion of labor flows is seen on this stage in redeveloping sphere and circulation sphere.

During this process, the labor flows are pursing translocation in three kinds of spaces: geographical, information-experience, structural-hierarchical ones. At each stage of given process it is necessary to comply with the requirements of logistics system seven rules. Labor flow dynamics in geographical space implies a consistent spatial motion of economically active population between educational institutions and enterprise-consumer of labor resources where their professional activity begins. Service sector specificity on this stage of labor flows dynamics is demonstrated by the absence of necessary number of educational institutions of specialized trends by kinds of service sector activities. Labor flow transfer on the stage of being in different educational institutions in structural-hierarchical space is almost not pursued except the case when social or political activities are held in parallel with the study. On this stage, foundations of further motion of labor flows are being laid therein. Motions in structural-hierarchical space are carried out most obviously in the process of labor flow potential implementation in various organizations. Translocations in information-experience space on the stage of forming of labor resource potential within educational institutions proceeds in parallel with geographical translocation but more intensively in time and by number of operations. Not only formation but also development of potential of labor resources, forming the labor flows, proceeds on subsequent stages of dynamics in information-experience space. Dynamics specificity of labor flows in information-experience space of the service sphere is shown in the need to combine several experience guidelines in the frames of one subject that gives possibility of further quicker transfer in structural-hierarchical space.

Labor flow dynamics on the level of organization includes personnel recruitment and placement, professional development, transfer to another workplace, mixing several functions within one position, new specialty training which purpose is to find optimal placement for employees in a team structure.

Sounds necessary to define correlation of information, financial and service flows of the service sector expressed in the usage of the value of profitable and expended financial flows for to estimate the coefficient of corresponding information flow: revenues, generated by information flows of service orders, exceed expenditures of these processes managing (Fig. 6.2). Other information flows, characterizing communication channels of service enterprise with market subjects and channels of necessary information acquisition, just indirectly participate in revenue formation.

Creation and consideration of logistic management system of service enterprise has its aim as optimization of resource usage, activity efficiency upturn, service quality improvement. Logistic system is formed on the basis of static and dynamic elements. Static elements, forming logistic system and determining its structure and form, are logistic system links, logistic chains, logistics networks, but flows form a dynamic basis being implemented in the form of flow processes.

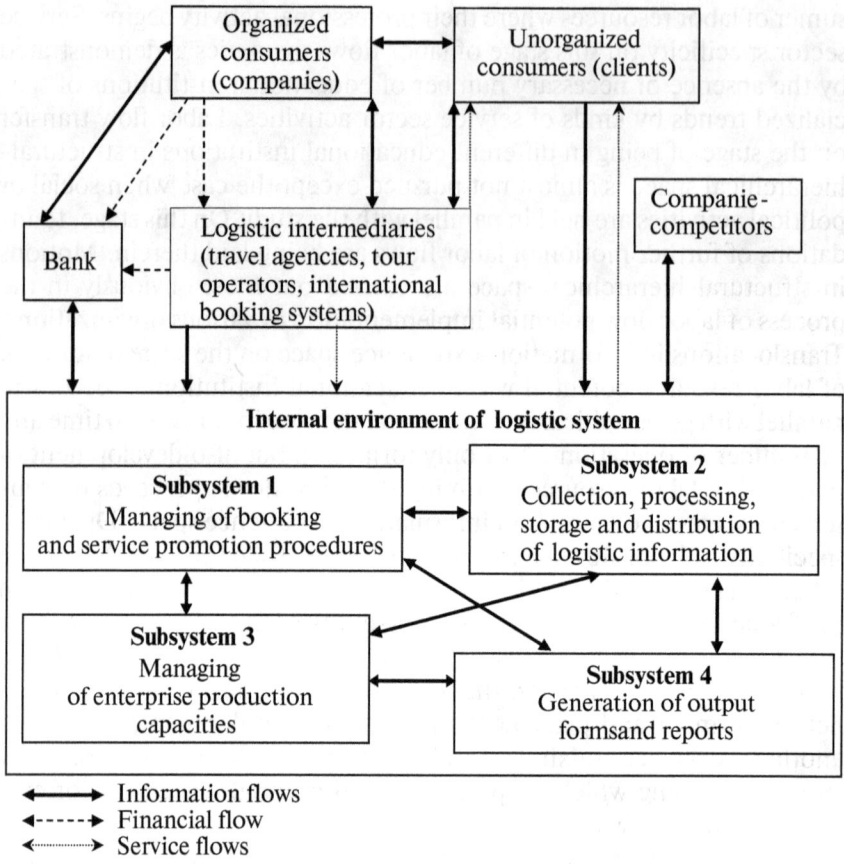

Figure 6.2. Structure of logistic system of service enterprise

The figure shows that four subsystems relate to logistic system internal environment, and organized and unorganized consumers, banks, competitors and intermediaries relate to the external environment. Information interaction of internal environment four subsystems determines the logistic activities of a service enterprise. One of the main functions of subsystem 3, affecting the parameters of internal resources in order to optimize them, is the planning of internal resources usage. Given subsystem causes direct impact on financial strategy of organization, on communicational, marketing activities, resource flows forecast and formation of effective enterprise management system.

Specificity of labor flows of service enterprise logistic system in organization's internal environment is revealed in the specifics of service itself, direct interaction with consumers, intermediaries, booking service and services promotion that should be considered herein.

Service enterprise management system includes the formation of a number of interconnected subsystems. It is possible to distinguish two main parts of governing system, one of which is a basic logistic part, the second is an operational one.

Basic logistics subsystem manages service enterprise resource flows. Operational part of management system consists of a set of three blocks created by imposition of management functions on enterprise organizational structure. Strategic management unit arranges management decisions of a strategic nature, the biggest unit of service production management is a specific area of service organization and performs the function of production process managing. Service production managing unit contains several major departments, nodes and subsystems — the subsystem of performance managing of new and existing service products, the subsystem of managing of procedures and technologies to promote services into market, the subsystem of managing of pre-orders formation, the subsystem of feedback formation on service results, the subsystem of management system information provision, the subsystem of managing of current orders provision and formation, the subsystem of managing of accounting and record operations at an enterprise, the subsystem of managing of organization's production capacities. Unit of production factors managing allows to rule personnel and material-technical base of an organization and represents the grounds for labor resources formation, allows to manage the dynamics and number of labor resources. Management system operational part is the basis for the formation and direct influence on organization's human resources, a basic logistic subsystem distributes and rules human resource flows of a service organization.

At the level of different types of resource flows in service enterprises, the prerequisites are being created for the construction of management logistic system of an organization on systematic approach basis. This management logistic system is a structured adaptive system consisting of elements connected by service and their accompanying financial and information flows. Creation and consideration of logistic system of service enterprise management is targeted at resource usage optimization, activities efficiency rise, service quality improvement. Organizational structure of logistic system in an enterprise is built basing on definition of information, financial and service flows. Information-based flow management remains a little-studied area of the service business.

On the basis of pursued analysis, sounds possible to make a conclusion about the necessity to apply integrated system approach to the management of a logistic system as a whole and to certain types of flow processes. The presence of not fully researched nodes of a logistic system of the service sector makes it necessary to further research in more details study of the issues.

REFERENCE LIST

1. Hesmondalgh D. 2014. Culture.
2. Fesel B., Sondermann M. 2007. Culture and Creative Industries in Germany // Bonn, 2007. p. 21
3. Malshina N.A. 2012. Theoretical Bases of Efficiency Increase of Functioning of Logistics Systems Flow Processes of Services Sector on the Basis of Traditional Concepts — Financial Flows // Proceedings of the Saratov University. Ser. Economy. Management.Right. 2012. Vol. 12., Vol. 1., pp. 72–76 *(in Russian)*.
4. Pontryagin L.S. 1974. Ordinary Differential Equations. 1974. M., Nauka*(in Russian)*.
5. Novikov D.T. 2012. Formation of Logistic Support in the Promotion of Scientific and Technical Developments / RISK. 2012. № 4, pp. 27 *(in Russian)*.
6. Malshina N.A., Bryntsev A.N. 2017. Support of Cultural Services through the Integrated Service Centers: Prospects for Development. Journal of Advanced Research in Law and Economics. Fall 2017. Volume VIII. Issue 6 (28).pp. 1827–1839.

7. INTERACTION OF DIGITAL ECONOMY AND LOGISTICS INNOVATIVE METHODS

Strategy for digital economy development, adopted in mid-2017 till 2020 [1], includes five main directions: "Information infrastructure", "Information security", "Personnel and education", "Policies and regulation" and "Formation of research competencies and technological grounds". Implementation of Program "Digital economy" assumes namely digitalization and wide introduction of information technologies as a condition of Russian economy growth. This strategy of information society development defines digital economy as economic activities wherein a key production factor are the data in digital form, the processing of large volumes, and which analyzed results usage, compared with traditional forms of economic management, allows to increase significantly the efficiency of various types of production, technologies, equipment, storage, sales, delivery of goods and services.

Objectives of Program "Digital Economy of the Russian Federation" [1], affirmed by decree of RF Government of July 28, 2017 No. 1632-R, are: "creation of an ecosystem of the digital economy of RF, wherein data in digital form is a key factor of production in all spheres of socio-economic activities, provided the effective interaction, including cross-border one, of business, of academic community, of states and citizens; the creation of necessary and sufficient conditions of institutional and infrastructural character; the elimination of existing obstacles and restrictions for creation and (or) development of high-tech businesses and the prevention emergence of new obstacles and restrictions both in traditional sectors of the economy and in new ones as well as in high-tech markets; the competitiveness rise on global market of both individual sectors of Russia economy and economy as a whole" [1].

The digital economy in RF is presented by the following three levels which, in their close interaction, affect citizen lives and society in a whole:
- markets and branches of economy (spheres of activity) where interaction of concrete subjects (suppliers and consumers of goods, works and services) is carried out;
- platforms and technologies where competencies are formed for the development of markets and industries (spheres of activity);
- an environment that creates conditions for the development of platforms and technologies and effective interaction of actors of markets

and economic sectors (spheres of activity) and covers norm regulation, information infrastructure, staff and information security; the development of Russia's digital economy is grounded on the main trends of the third and fourth industrial revolutions.

The introduction of information technologies into all modern branches of RF economy takes place in the form of new business models, leads to the formation of large information data arrays. Basing on official statistics, we can say that the penetration of information technologies and the digitalization process of economy proceeds towards different directions in economy various sectors at present in Russia (Table 7.1).

2011 is a breaking point which after negative dynamics started for many industries. However, such areas as e-mailing and global information networks, Internet demonstrate positive dynamics so far that implies the presence of necessary potential for full digitization of RF economy. Deep penetration of technologies creates prerequisites for the use of relevant data for the assessment and forecasting of economic development.

The use of advanced production technologies across subjects of the Russian Federation clearly demonstrates a steady positive trend. Developed advanced production technologies across Russian Federation subjects demonstrate multidirectional dynamics: across the Russian Federation in a whole — a stable positive dynamics.

As it can be seen, the development of advanced production technologies by RF subjects has certain bars but the use of the technologies does not meet significant obstacles.

One of the main directions of the digital economy development is the presence of high-performance jobs by various kinds of economic activities.

Digital innovations in a narrow sense refer to the introduction of a new or significantly improved product of information-communication technologies (ICT; product or service), i.e. innovation products in ICT sphere; more broadly — refer to the use of ICT for the introduction of a new or significantly improved product, process, marketing method or organizational method, i.e. innovations with the using of ICT.

According to BCG (Boston Consulting Group), the main digital economies in the world include South Korea, Germany, Sweden, Japan and Switzerland: the share of the digital economy in the GDP of developed countries is 5.5%, developing countries — 4.9%. According to "Runet Economy 2015-2016" in Russia, the share of the digital economy in GDP is 2.4% (the volume of Runet economy (content and services) at the end of 2015 amounted to 1,355. 38 billion rubles, and the volume of electronic payments market — to 588 billion rubles).

Table 7.1. Use of information and communication technologies in organizations

	Organizations that have used								
	personal computers		servers		local computer networks		global information networks	including Internet	
	2017	2018	2017	2018	2017	2018	2017	2018	2017
Total	92.1	94.0	50.6	53.4	61.1	63.9	89,7	92.0	88.9
Construction	88.9	86.1	58.0	53.9	59.9	55.4	87.1	84.1	86.5
Wholesale and retail trade; vehicle and motorcycle repairment	94.3	95.1	64.3	66.3	72.1	73.8	93.5	94.3	92.6
Transportation and storage	93.4	92.7	58.2	57.6	73.0	71.9	91.7	91.2	84.7
Hotels and catering organization activities	90.3	88.5	50.6	48.7	53.1	53.0	86.0	85.2	85.7
Activities in information and communication sphere	97.0	96.4	63.5	63.1	71.6	69.5	95.7	95.3	94.9
of these in telecommunication sphere	96.4	94.1	80.1	73.2	85.2	80.5	95.0	9,,8	93.6
Financial and insurance activities	94.9	96.0	53.4	52.6	73.8	75.3	92,4	95.2	92.2
Real estate activities	65.6	86.4	21.9	43.0	23.0	46.4	62.6	84.1	62.3
Professional, scientific and technical activities	93.1	92.3	52.6	52.2	61.4	59.4	91.1	90.6	90.7
of these, research and inventions	96.2	94.5	70.4	66.3	74.8	71.0	94.9	92.5	94.5
Administrative activities and related additional services	89.7	89.2	57.3	54.8	62.1	60.0	86.6	85.6	86.0
Public administration and military security provision; social security	97.2	97.2	46.3	47.2	62.4	62.4	95.0	95.1	94.6
Higher education; training of highly qualified personnel	98.4	96.8	84.2	71.1	90.6	78.1	97.1	95.5	97.1

Table 7.1 completion

| | Organizations that have used | | | | | | | | |
| | personal computers | | servers | | local computer networks | | global information networks | including Internet | |
	2017	2018	2017	2018	2017	2018	2017	2018	2017
Activities in the field of health and social services provision	96.8	97.1	62.6	63.2	78.6	78.9	95.0	95.5	94.9
Activities in the field of culture, sports, leisure and entertainment	91.1	91.9	23.4	24.1	35.4	35.7	84.5	86.3	84.4
Repairment of computers, personal belongings and household appliances	93.5	83.9	62.9	31.4	77.2	62.2	92.4	82.2	85.3
Activity other kinds	94.0	93.0	39.4	38.1	56.6	57.6	91.2	90.6	91.2
Collective classificational grouping of economic activities kinds "Sector of engineering services and industrial design"	95.1	93.0	68.1	69.1	78.5	76.4	94.7	92.5	94.7
Collective classification grouping of economic activities kinds "Sector of information-communicational technologies"	96.7	94.7	78.0	72.0	83.8	78.6	95.7	93.7	93.9
Collective classification grouping of economic activities kinds "Sector of content and mass media"	97.3	97.5	42.9	45.9	55.2	54.5	95.5	96.2	95.5
Collective classification grouping of economic activities kinds "Information technology industry"	97.1	97.5	77.3	77.2	84.1	81.0	96.4	96.8	95.0

Beijing declared at the end of 2016 that China had reached the second place in the world in terms of level and scale of development of so-called digital economy. In particular, China hosted Forum on Digital

Economy Issues in the frames of Third World Conference on Management of Internet in November. As RenXulin, Director of State Office for Internet-Information Affairs, said at the forum, the scale of China's digital economy in 2015 was estimated at 18.6 trillion. yuanes (about 2.7 trillion US dollars or almost 14% of China's GDP). The assessment is rather relative, since there are no established and reliable methods for calculating the size of digital economy sector.

E-commerce accounted for 8.4% of China's total retail turnover and accounted for about 55% of all turnovers on China's digital market in 2014 according to BCG. Higher relative values were marked only in the UK (11.4%) and Germany (10.2%), they were lower (respectively 6.8 and 6.2%) in countries such as the US and Japan. However, digital economy other elements in China are less developed than in the US and EU countries. We are talking, in particular, about electronic banking, electronic payments, etc.

The inclusion of new direction "Digital Transport and Logistics" in the program "Digital Economy" in near future is discussed. "Digital Logistics" arises in response to global challenges of the digital economy for traditional transport and logistics sector, such as rapidly changing globalized and highly competitive trading environment, supply chain complexity, rapid change in customer expectations, infrastructure limited resources.

Taking into account that state budget still remains the main source of culture's existence, direct budget distribution still prevails, it seems necessary to provide for the possibility of projects financing on digitization in culture sphere at the legislative level through mechanisms of public-private partnership, interaction and coordination of federal and regional public development institutions. Digitalization in the culture sphere has potential for attraction of income new sources into the culture sphere, for provision of investments attraction to the sphere [2].

Problems of logistics in e-commerce are connected primarily with faster pace of formation and implementation of supply chains of goods compared to traditional trade. This feature of e-commerce determines the need to improve the mechanisms of demand forecast that should contribute to a more rational planning of the stock of goods in warehouses in various geographical regions, reducing the time of goods turnover and delivery cost.

E-commerce is a significant institution of the digital economy, goes into an increasing number of legal relations, emerging in the field of trade, and covers all spectrum of relations — immediate interaction of consumers with consumers (C2C), interaction of sellers with consumers (B2C), interaction between entrepreneurs (B2B), interaction of business and government in electronic form (B2G) and others.

It is necessary to develop and introduce data analysis technologies on demand for the distribution logistics planning frames of the e-commerce development. At the same time, in the "B2B" sector (Business to Business), it may be promising to introduce technologies, including those that use achievements allowing self-monitoring of up-to-date information about a proposal, tracking of a production cycle that will allow to carry out more effective planning of purchases and their logistic support accordingly.

The Decree of the President of the Russian Federation [1] states tasks on that "primacy in research and development, a high rate of development of new knowledge and creation of innovative products are the key factors determining the competitiveness of national economies and the effectiveness of national security strategy." This is achieved to large extent due to: "the connectivity of RF territory through the creation of intellectual transport systems as well as the occupation and retention of leadership positions in the creation of international transport systems" [2]. Of course, highly developed and modern transport and logistic systems today are key factors in country economic competitiveness. Maintenance and improvement of efficient transport and logistic infrastructures for resource flow motion continue to stay important in today's national and global markets, especially given the projected population growth and the inevitable drastic changes in industry, energetics (especially in oil and gas sectors) and agriculture production [7, p. 50].

Systemic and institutional problems pose serious barriers to the development of innovations in logistics. Among them — inconsistency of actions of numerous authorized institutions, lack of scientifically grounded programs of development and of accurate, thought-over priorities, low level of administration, irrational and inefficient distribution of budgetary funds, voluntarism, opaque and inappropriate financing, domination of bureaucratic structures subordinating science to their own interests, lack of competence, personnel shortage, non-involvement of SMEs (Small and Middle-sized Enterprises) into innovations. We arrive at a conclusion coinciding with statements of independent experts on the need for root institutional changes in science and innovation management, wider freedom for entrepreneurial initiative [4, p. 90].

Logistics in the digital economy creates intellectual mobility as a new industry which integrates both the motion of physical objects and human flows that requires serious transformations for future supply chains.

According to the results of the Parliamentary hearings in the State Duma of the Federal Assembly of the Russian Federation on the topic "Formation of legal conditions for financing and development of the digital economy" (February 20, 2018) [6], further prospects for the development of RF digital economy 'in the field of logistics are proposed: the most rapid transition to fully electronic interaction in all formats: B2B, B2C, B2G, C2G (access expansion of financial organizations to state information resources, storage and use of legally significant electronic documents, legally significant digitization of paper documents, use expansion of simple and strengthened expertise electronic signatures in protected environments). However, general trends of digital economy further development cause straight impact on logistic activities: financial infrastructure development; research and working-out of proposals on application of novel financial technologies (including Big Data and Smart Data, artificial intelligence, machine learning, distributed Ledger technology, open interfaces (Open API (Application Programming Interface)); creation of test regulatory platforms ("sandbox") on the basis of the Bank of Russia; formation of a single payment space within the EAEU; ensuring security and sustainability while application of financial technologies; personnel development in the field of financial technologies.

The application of logistic methods in the digital economy in the culture field ensures the active involvement into a target audience of cultural institutions of a new generation, focused mainly on the digital format of perception of available information.

Such, in the Belgorod region, the project on creation of a common information infrastructure in the field of culture and tourism "Cultural region" has been implemented presuming high-quality media content (photos and videos), performance of a regional ticketing system: e-tickets — to all cultural institutions of the region (in accordance with the Federal Law No. 54), permanent training of employees in the culture sphere, formation of a uniform cultural space of the region, promotion of a cultural product in Internet and urban environment, introduction of modern technologies for a culture product promotion. In the framework of pilot stage implementation of the project for 2017, audit of the industry condition in the region was conducted, more than 500 employees of cultural institutions had passed the training. more than 200 hours of video content, 3,000 photos, documentary had been created, website, mobile application had been launched, online cashboxes had been turned on, testing of the new formats had been carried out: quests, streaming to the audience of more than 1.5 million people, offline activities: festivals, quiz programs etc., a growth in Russia Culture Ministry ranking (the First place) had been made. This project had proved in practice the effectiveness of cultural services digitalization, assuming the return in the form of human flows of consumers and, hence, reverse financial flows. 2018 development plan already included the close interaction of cultural services and tourist services aimed at attendance increasing of cultural institutions and ticket sales, the development of non-cash forms of payment and the application of CRE (Cash Register Equipment) in accordance with Federal law No. 54:

1. Cultural-tourist center launch;
2. Single ticket to cultural institutions;
3. Start of a mass sale of electronic tickets;
4. Creation of a database of contacts of the audience of cultural events;
5. Formation of package offers for residents and guests of the city;
6. Ratio increase for electronic tickets and non-cash payment.

Digitalization in the culture sphere should provide for the development of new directions of intrinsic and inbound tourism through the optimization of activities in the sphere of use and preservation of the cultural heritage of Russian Federation peoples.

"Museum in the Era of Digital Transformation" represents an embodied project of the culture sphere digitization on the example of the Pushkin state Museum of Fine Arts with a total storage capacity of more than 671,000 units, 350,00 volumes in the library (rare books constitute 10%), 800,000 units of archival materials [3]. As a part of the implementation of this project in 2017, the total number of visitors to the exposition, exhibitions and events of the Museum was 1,300,000 people, website visitors were more than 4,000,000, social media subscribers were more than 400,000. As a result of the activity, the main directions of IT usage in museum sphere were fulfilled:

1. Design and modernization of CS (Client Service), integrated management systems, IT infrastructure (LAN; data centers; storages; system, server and client software);
2. Integrated security and monitoring systems (video surveillance, DMCS (Diagnostics Monitoring and Control System), etc.);
3. Digitization of collections, automated accounting systems of funds and digital resources storage;
4. Efficiency improvement (Corporate portal, electronic document management system)4

5. Virtual/information space of a museum (websites, virtual museums, social networks, VR, etc.);
6. Services and products implementation system, ESVKC (Electronic Signature Verification Key Certificate), e-commerce, loyalty programs and CRM (Customer Relationship Management) system, business analytics, marketing video analytics;
7. IT accompaniment of architectural and exposition design (visualization, etc.);
8. Multimedia in exposition and exhibition projects, IT application in educational activities, implementation of the project of electronic lectures and media representations;
9. Research and experimental application of new technologies.

For the formation of knowledge information space in the culture sphere, it is necessary, inter alia:

• to form an accessible and secure database of culture information resources which promote the spread of traditional Russian spiritual-moral values;
• to improve mechanisms for knowledge and tradition exchange;
• to provide formation of a National electronic library and other state information systems that should include objects of historical, scientific and cultural heritage of Russian Federation peoples as well as to provide their access by maximally wide user range;
• to create conditions for Russian culture and science popularization abroad including for the purpose of counteraction to attempts of historical and other facts distortion and falsification;
• to take measures for the effective usage of modern information platforms for the spread of reliable and high-quality information of Russian production;
• to ensure market saturation with affordable, high-quality and legal media products and services of Russian production.

According to the results of Parliamentary hearings in the State Duma of Federal Assembly of the Russian Federation on topic "Formation of legal conditions for financing and development of digital economy" (February 20, 2018) [6], further development prospects of RF digital economy in the culture field suggest: the most rapid transition to fully electronic interaction by all formats (access expansion of financial organizations to state information resources, storage and use of legally significant electronic documents, legally significant digitization of documents on paper, increase of usage of simple and enhanced protection of authorized electronic signatures in secure environments). Logistics in the digital economy of the culture services sector creates intellectual mobility as a new industry which combines both physical objects motion and people flows, cultural values in information space that requires major transformations for supply chains of all kinds of resources.

But real digital economy — is the economy of platforms, which also answers the question posed by the head of the trade Union movement. "Platform — is a system of relations between a consumer (citizen), who is guaranteed to receive a quality service at a fixed price, and those who offer this service and are guaranteed to receive appropriate payment for it, and state and society, which receive corresponding tax and social deductions" [7].

This is fundamentally important because it brings up those who are now in a shadow and forms accordingly a normal transparent system without disproportions in concurrence.

Vital need in formation of strategic directions of development of a culture industry business entity is due to the fact that state regulation of the sphere cannot be carried out without understanding further direction of logistic approach development. In addition, none business entity in a market economy can be effective if it has not developed a set of measures to achieve the goals.

However, general tendencies of further development of the digital economy in RF culture sphere assume later on: development of financial infrastructure of the culture sphere (study and elaboration of proposals on application of novel financial technologies); development of testing regulatory cultural courts on the basis of RF Culture Ministry; formation of a single payment space in EAEU framework; security and sustainability provision in financial technologies application; personnel development. Modern digital logistic approaches in the culture field require the effective management of financial flows, state information and legislative support, highly qualified personnel provision.

REFERENCE LIST

1. Decree of the President of the Russian Federation "On Strategy of Scientific-Technological Development of RF" dated December 1, 2016 No. 642 // Administration of the President of Russia 2018. http://www.kremlin.ru/acts/bank/41449 *(in Russian)*.
2. Kupriyanovskii V.Yu. et al. Information Technologies in the System of Universities, Science and Innovation in Digital Economy on UK Example / / International Journal of Open Information Technologies. — 2016. — V. 4. — No. 4. — Pp. 30–39.

3. Katasonov V.Yu. On China Digital Economy // VseSovetnik, online magazine. http://www.vsesovetnik.ru/archives/22055 *(in Russian)*.
4. Garnov A.P., Garnova V.Yu. Innovative Potential of Russia: Problems and Prospects of Realization // RISK: Resources, Information, Supply, Competition. — 2016. — No. 1. Pp. 92-97 *(in Russian)*..
5. Science, innovation and Informational Society // Federal State Statistics Service / URL: /http://www.gks.ru/wps/wcm/connect/rosstat_main/rosstat/ru/statistics/science_and_innovations/science/# *(in Russian)*.
6. Materials for the Parliamentary Hearings on February 20, 2018 on "Formation of Legal Conditions for Financing and Development of Digital Economy" // State Duma Committee on Financial Market / URL: http://komitet2-12.km.duma.gov.ru/Novosti-Komiteta/item/15619340 *(in Russian)*.
7. Garnov A.P., Kireeva N.S. Financial, Material and Information Flows: Point of Interaction in Logistics // RISK: Resources, Information, Supply, Competition. — 2017. — No. 2. Pp. 48-51 *(in Russian)*.

8. APPLICATION OF STRATEGIC PLANNING METHOD FOR FLOW PROCESSES MANAGEMENT OF CULTURE INDUSTRY

Practice shows that culture sphere management in modern market conditions presents significant difficulties. Strategic goals and objectives occur that socio-cultural organizations did not solve previously themselves and did not set up initially. All occurring problems associated with these goals and objectives cannot be solved without effective logistics-oriented management.

Management of social and cultural institution internal environment implies the implementation of all major traditional functions. During the implementation of given functions in accordance with the requirements of logistics, a development strategy and tactics should be worked out, strategic and operational goals should be defined as well as measures should be held for to achieve these goals.

In terms of technology, the management process represents itself primarily an organizational procedures and operations related to the obtaining, storage and processing of a variable information. In general view, a management is the process of influencing a system for transferring it into a new state or its maintaining in some given mode. Logistics management implies "maximally high level of coordination of all flow processes of resources " [2].

Logistics concept requires the implementation of integrated management and regulation of moving and usage of resource flow processes, the account of specifics of socio-cultural services provided for and consumed by a consumer. In order the logistics to meet the requirements of cultural industry management, the planning and practical activities process must comply with the demands of accessibility and ability of information submission at different levels. The implementation of these requirements will allow to improve management control, to conduct operational and strategic activities analysis.

According to expert estimates, the direct costs of logistics and logistics services in many European countries constitute about 8-14% of GDP (France: 10%, Germany: 7.8%, EU as a whole: 13.3%) with an upward trend. Logistics accounts for 6-12% of workforce to total number of employees.

The experience of Western European countries shows the significant role of LC in budgeting and reducing the overall logistics costs of consumers. Thus, in the Netherlands, the activity of transit LC brings 40% of the transport complex income, in France — 31%, in Germany — 25%. In the countries of Central and Eastern Europe, this percent constitutes 30 percent in average. So, in a whole, the total turnover of the European logistics services market reaches more than 600 billion Euros. Of these.about 30% of logistics functions in all sectors of the economy are given to logistics companies annually, many of which exploit LC services. According to European Logistics Association, usage of LC in supply chains during implementing the transportation multi-modal technologies allows clients to save 12–15% of the delivery cost in the direct mixed traffic. While such logistical functions were passed to LC outsourcing most often as:

- warehousing — 73,7%;
- external transportation — 68.4%;
- cargo execution/payments arrangement — 61,4%;
- internal transportation — 56,1%;
- cargoes consolidation/distributions — 40.4%;
- direct transportation — 38.6% [2].

Along with obvious differences between Europe LCs, there are several common features such as multi-modality stimulation, procurement of incentives for transition from one transportation kind to another, openness, accessibility and multi-user approach as a requirement for neutral developers/ operators. These characteristics can also serve as success criteria which make it possible to respond flexibly to market conditions changes in connection with political goals implementation.

In market conditions, any field of activity operates in an environment where dynamic changes are undergoing constantly. The list of factors, influencing the company.changes. Over time, the influence of some factors intensifies while, of others, weakens. On the one hand, the ongoing changes create favorable conditions for a company and open up new opportunities. On the other hand, unfavorable circumstances and additional restrictions occur. So, for to work out an optimal strategy development for culture sphere business entity the environment current state of its functioning must be researched and the threats and the new opportunities must be identified.

For this task settlement, such method of strategic planning as SWOT-analysis can be used. It enables to establish links between strengths and weaknesses, that are inherent to companies, and external factors: threats and opportunities. This method choice for prospects forecast of business entity functioning development is due to its versatility and relative ease to hold. It seems to us that SWOT-analysis application for exposure of regularities of economic mutual relations on Russian market is rightful both for an individual enterprise and for their groups combined according to a row of common features.

Methodology of SWOT-analysis realization implies first the clarification of company strengths and weaknesses, of its external threats and opportunities. After that, analysis of links between them is carried out for to use them further to determine company's development strategy. Next stage, business entity management team, having studied the potential risks and opening prospects, accepts decisions on the necessity of carrying out one or another actions.

By the way of management object in logistics component of culture sphere the flow processes of resources (material, informational, financial) are considered. The task of the logistics is in that to interlink organizational, technological, economic, social interests and those ones of all participants of resources movement process as of an integral system. "Activities rationalization of logistics chain individual links or their combination following a certain algorithm represents itself an optimization goal "[1].

When managing a specific business structure of socio-cultural service sector, the application of logistics approach to the logistics system each element is improved in a necessary scope at a necessary location and a time. As a result of paid services structure of Russia, the household, transport, communications and medical services have the biggest percentage.

However, the aspect of this approach application in the culture and art services sphere remains poorly researched, although it has a clear specificity. In the light of modern global informational technologies and digitalization in service, it seems necessary to expand research scope onto services sphere and particularly onto culture services sphere.

However, initially, the system data are created for the financial accounting which implicates the absence of services volume indicators of culture and of culture and creativity products in the culture industries frames in the informational system. "To settle these shortcomings a company needs to reduce the accounting and financial sector impact and to divide given areas in logistics and other ones" [3]. Documents passing to other departments should be established by electronic exchange, such transactions should be included in the system that would allow for accounting office to see electronic versions onto each product, grocery or culture service. Culture service calculation should be counted accordingly the one-time issue and production.

Condition	
Strength	*Weakness*
• the presence of a permanent market; • availability of production and equipment and machinery; • professional staff; • close links with local government and control; • relatively stable financial position	• insufficient financing; • usual organizational methods and management style; • insufficient attention to retraining; • insufficient attention to marketing strategy

Outlook	
Opportunity*:	*Threats*:*
• social and economic policy ofthe state; • state support for the development of the industry; • the emergence of new production technologies; • attracting investors and establishing more effective partnerships	• the deterioration of macro-economic support; • significant proportion of low-income families; • negative population growth; • changing consumer preferences
* external environment	

Figure 8.1. Extended list of strengths and weaknesses of business entities as well as of opportunities and threats from the external environment side

The extended list of strengths and weaknesses for business entities as well as of threats and opportunities for them from the side of business-surrounding is presented on Fig. 8.1.

Each particular company, surely, can add or cut the list with those characteristics of the external and internal environment which reflect its real situation.

After arranging of the list of weaknesses and strengths of business entities as well as of threats and opportunities arising for them, it is necessary to find the connections between them. To do this it is feasibly to distribute them according the following matrix (Fig. 8.2):

Outlook / Condition	Opportunity	Threats
Strength	A	C
Weakness	B	D

Figure. 8.2. Matrix of opportunities and threats analysis for business entity amid strength and weakness of their positions.

The two sections which are on the matrix left part (strengths, weaknesses) for business entity with all main strengths and weaknesses identified at the analysis first stage. The two sections at the matrix top (opportunities and threats) are filled in with all main opportunities and threats.

The following fields are formed at sections crossing: field "A" (strength and opportunities); field "B" (weakness and opportunities); field "C" (strength and threats); field "D" (weakness and threats). During the analysis, it is necessary to identify on each of the four fields the paired combinations which should be taken into account further in a course of the working out of principal approaches of the development strategy definition. The cells with the biggest interaction power between the most influential factors are studied herewith.

For combinations that on the "A" field, it is needed to mastermind a strategy of strengths usage for a business entity in order to take full advantage of the opportunities appeared in the external environment. The strategy for combinations located on the "B" field should be composed in a way to try overcoming or minimizing the weaknesses that enterprise has at the expense of the appeared opportunities. For combinations that occurred on "C" field, a strategy is needed that is aimed at company strengths usage for to eliminate threats arising in its external environment and for to neutralize them. If conjunction is on "D" field the situation is crisis-ridden because environment threats and company weakness conjoin here. The strategy in this situation will be connected with attempts to get rid of both weaknesses and external threats. An example of such a strategy is a concentration on a market narrow segment.

Implementation of the chosen strategy proceeds on the next step. It includes organizational -economic, coordinating and controlling actions, which result in that business entities gradually modify their structure, resources, forms and work methods, orientating on the model of future behavior defined by the strategy of its development.

The strategy is implemented at management various levels, while the strategy implementation and its implementation monitoring demonstrate the greatest efficiency when using logistics informational systems. In turn, the informational environment also requires the management both at the level of individual business entity and at the level of national economy as a whole.

Modern economic space is becoming informational-digital in all its branches. It is to obtain the service when it is needed and not to spend much time on it. Service sector and, in particular.the culture industry based on direct contact of consumer and producer gets possibility to minimize costs according to the use of informational technology. Consumers receive a variety of goods and services, and manufacturers — feedback from buyers.

Today, the "digital economy is about 4% of GDP" [4] that is 2–3 times less than ones in the countries-leaders, and on the one hand, we are very well behind, but on the other hand, we have a potential, opportunities for a serious development.

The logistics in the digital economy of the culture services sphere creates intellectual mobility as a new industry which combines displacement of physical objects as well as of human flows, cultural values in informational space that demands serious transformations for supply chains of all resource types.

However, general trends of digital economy further development in culture sphere of Russian Federation in future suggest: financial infrastructure development of the culture sphere (research and development of proposals for the use of novel financial technologies); creation of trial regulatory cultural sites on the basis of Russian Federation Culture Ministry; formation of a single payment space within EEU; security and sustainability provision during the use of financial technologies; personnel development [5]. Modern digital logistics approaches in the culture field demand effective management of financial flows, state informational and legislative support, highly qualified staff provision.

Digital economy logistics of culture services sphere is important primarily because it involves in the digital economy a large number of new consumers, citizens [6]. Without the obligatory involvement of citizens into the digital economy, we will certainly fall behind as consumers, and by these means the business will be in insufficient degree demand. At the same time, we understand that this work does not form a digital economy, it forms economy that is a digitized.

The urgent need for the formation of development strategic directions of culture industry business entity is connected with that the given sphere state regulation is impossible to be held without understanding of development further direction of the logistics approach. In addition, none business entity in a market-driven economy can be effective if it has not developed measures complex on goals achievement.

The logistics methods application should be one of the most important goals in the formation of the system of socio-cultural services in Russia. Long-term logistics partnership in the socio-cultural services sector is preferable for the following reasons: allows to create sustainable channels for the advanced knowledge passing; modern organizational and technological breakthroughs, including logistics ones, are formed on sciences or industries intersection; joint elaborations and innovational projects allow to reduce the costs and risks of integration process. In this case, a trust acts as an economic factor providing for a centeredness of development and competitive advantages to all participants of socio-cultural services logistics system. Principle of targeting, involving the determination of activities direction towards certain groups of microeconomic systems against the needs in specific services and the implementation within specific models, underlies the practical implementation of management logistics methods in the culture sphere. This principle also implies the development of a system of state guarantees for the cultural services.

Activity results find direct reflection in actual amount of costs referred to operational tasks fulfillment. Expected costs definition constitutes the essence of budget planning. Logistics costs amount is made of either by costs overall monetary amount or by monetary amount per product unit (costs per unit), or by sales volume share.

Thus, in the management of business-structures of socio-cultural services, it is necessary to consider them in the unity and the integrity of their components which are inextricably connected with the outside world.

REFERENCE LIST

1. Garnov A.P., Kireeva N.C. Strategic Planning and Management as a Basis of Business Value Increase by Multi-link Logistics Chains // Logistics. 2012. № 1 (62). — pp. 20–23.
2. Garnov A.P., Kireeva N.C. Logistics Tools: Monograph. 2nd edition, added // M: INFRA-M, 2017. — 254 p.
3. The Order of the Ministry of Culture of the Russian Federation of June 28, 2013 N 920 "About Approval of Methodical Recommendations on Development by Public Authorities of Russian Federation

Subjects and by Local Governments of Indicators for Efficiency Activity of Subordinated Culture Institutions, their Heads and Workers by Organization Types and Workers Major Categories" — URL: http://www.garant.ru/products/ipo/prime/doc/70327762/#ixzz4nejrFzSc (application date 12.06.2017) *(in Russian)*.

4. Socio-economic situation in Russia — 2017 / Federal State Statistics Service-URL: http://www.gks.ru/bgd/regl/b17_01/Main.htm (application date 12. 06.2017) *(in Russian)*.

5. State Duma of the Federal Assembly of the Russian Federation // Culture Committee [electronic resource] — access mode — URL: http://komitet2-3.km.duma.gov.EN/upload/site16/Opredelenov. pdf *(in Russian)*.

6. Materials on Parliamentary Hearings on February 20, 2018 on "Formation of Legal Conditions for Financing and Development of Digital Economy" // State Duma Committee of Financial Market [electronic resource] — access mode — URL: http://komitet2-12. km.duma.gov.ru/Novosti-Komiteta/item/15619340 *(in Russian)*.

CONCLUSION

As a result of the study, the objectives were achieved. The integrated approach makes it possible to combine functional areas of the logistics by coordinating actions performed by independent parts of the logistics system, sharing common responsibility within the target function.The theory and practice of foreign companies proves the effectiveness of this approach in resource management. The use of the basic statements of the logistics approach as well as of individual logistics principles to improve the efficiency of economic resources management will allow the possibility of increasing the logistics systems stability of the service and tourism sector by the way of their closer interaction through integration both in the logistics chain itself and with the dynamic external environment.

The modern concept of resource management leans on strategic management which is aimed, among other things, at the formation of an innovative culture in a company (we mean a stable set of certain type abilities). The culture of innovations comes into being as a result of the implementation of an innovation strategy of which the main elements are: focus on the customer (the creation of a system of continuous monitoring of customer satisfaction and the adaptation of a company to changes in customers' preferences, the analysis of the long-term development of needs and providing for an advanced development of the product or service);leadership of managers; employees involvement in the generation of innovation;implementation of continuous improvements (kaizen); application of a process approach for operational control.

All the prerequisites of the formation of an innovative culture of economic entities are created in supply chains today. It becomes possible to focus on the consumer due to tight integration, because the modern logistics concept of the creation of added value puts the consumer first. At the same time, the innovative mechanism of logistics tools enables the forecasting of consumer preferences development, science and technology development, and market opportunities. The use of the logistics management tools in the service sector also shows innovation.

In the conditions of profound economic crisis, issues of the effective management of resource potential and, therefore the rational use of resources, come to the fore. The logistics mobilization of all managing reserves is of particular importance for the social-cultural services sphere at the present stage of market relations in Russia. The resource saving for the rapidly developing services sector of Russia will boost competitiveness in the world market.

The culture industry support for and the formation of organizational-economic mechanism for managing the given process are particularly vital for the Russian economy because of the presence of significant untapped reserves, potential opportunities for the effective application of logistic approach and of integrating strategies formation.

Financing methods of innovative design in the culture field are possible as a technology to maintain the cultural services' variety, their market demand boost that allows to embody tight dependence of financing purpose from activities results. Main directions of the reform of culture services' backing system — are inter-industries and inter-budgetary relations of the culture sphere in the frames of various activity kinds.

Based on the usage analysis of tools of endowment, public-private partnership, guarantee schemes and other financial-credit mechanisms and innovative funding tools in the culture industry, the concept of integrated service complexes models in the culture industry is masterminded as a mechanism for development and support of the culture industry in Russia regions, grounded on backing different models.

Application of the current study results in the form of large-scale creation and in the form of financing mechanisms introduction is of high applied significance and that will allow:

- to expand culture institutions client contacts on the backs of market new segments development of the culture services industry which will enhance consumption volume of held services and of culture industry subjects' income on integration basis;
- to provide citizens with demanded services, to develop the culture industry infrastructure;
- to optimize the state budget expenditures towards the culture industry services formation and development from public-private partnership utilization in this sphere;
- to create favorable conditions for investments attracting into services sphere in a whole and into the culture industry;
- to reduce the risk degree of entry of the culture industry services into consumer's new markets;
- to heighten the profitability of the culture industry functioning by the way of providing an open access to culture services information and major characteristics.

Strategic planning methods usage presupposes innovative activities, business-processes logistization, structural-functional and other changes necessary to adapt to external environment impacts.

The changing logistic potential of an activity subject shows a delayed and weakened response to positive impacts, in contrast to the influence of destructive factors having a rapid effect.

Thus, in the business-structures management of social-cultural services, it is necessary to consider them in the unity and integrity of the components which are inextricably linked to the outside world.

Further global integration of society, culture and business requires new mechanisms to provide for the creative industry development in Russia with account of development world experience, maximization of resource potential usage and adoption of management verified organizational-economic mechanisms for the development of the culture industry.

Currently, the underdevelopment of organizational-economic forms and insufficient elaboration of mechanisms for support and strategic development of the creative industry hampers this sphere evolution, and the structure of investment sources of RF socio-cultural projects reveals a disproportion between public and private sectors and asymmetry between needs and opportunities for pointed projects financing.

The formation of logistization optimal mode of the creative industry with its subsequent adjustment in accordance with structural and market changes is the content of operational organizational work. Together, the essence of logistization process management is mainly defined by sectoral priorities in region, i.e. that is specific in terms of implementation ways and methods. In its turn, the creation of favorable conditions for capital investment into region economy infrastructure sector, as a material base of socio-cultural service sphere, is a strategic organizational direction of general character.

The integrated paradigm provides an opportunity to increase the stability of logistic systems by ensuring their closer interaction that requires further integration both in logistics chain itself and with dynamic external environment. At the same time, to solve these tasks the traditional paradigm is not enough as a rule. Therefore, in the current conditions, the integral paradigm of logistics becomes particularly relevant providing a synthesis of elements of logistic system integrated on the basis of material, labor and other logistics flow that implies a new scheme of interaction.

Vital need in formation of strategic directions of development of a culture industry business entity is due to the fact that state regulation of the sphere cannot be carried out without understanding further direction of logistic approach development. In addition, none business entity in a market economy can be effective if it has not developed a set of measures to achieve the goals.

REFERENCE LIST

1. Adler N.J. International Dimensions of Organizational Behavoir. Boston: PWS-Kent Publishing Company. 1991. 313 p.
2. Adorno T.W. Culture Industry reconsidered, in The Culture Idustry / Witkin R.W. Adorno on popular Culture. Cambridge: Polity, 2003. 385 p.
3. Alden D.L., Hoyer W.D., & Lee C. Identifying global and culture specific dimensions of humor in advertising: A multinational analysis // Journal of Marketing, 1993. № 57. P. 64–75.
4. Barro R.J., McCleary R. Religion and Economic Growth across Countries. American Sociological Association, 2003, 68(5). Pp. 760–781.
5. Benjamin V. Work of Art in the Era of its Technical Reproducibility // Moscow: Goethe Cultural Center; Medium 1996. P. 196 (*in Russian*).
6. Bernstein J. M. Introduction to Adorno's the culture industry. London and New York. 2008. 210 p.
7. Bourbieu P. The Field of cultural production: essays on art and literature. Cambridge: Polity press. 1993. 321 p.
8. Bowersox D.J., Closs D.J., Helferich O.K. Logistical Management. McMillan Publishing, 3rd. 1991.
9. Cooper J. European Logistics / J. Cooper, M. Browne, M. Peters. Oxford: Blackwell Publishers, 1991.
10. Decree of the President of the Russian Federation "On Strategy of Scientific-Technological Development of RF" dated December 1, 2016. No. 642 // Administration of the President of Russia 2018. URL: http://www.kremlin.ru/acts/bank/41449 (*in Russian*).
11. Effectiveness of Logistics Management: Textbook for High Schools // Under editorship of L.B. Mirotin. M.: Publishing house "Examination", 2004. 448 pp.
12. Exploring the Northern Dimension, available at: http://www.ndinstitute.org.
13. Fernandez R. Women, work, and culture // Journal of the European Economic Association, 2008. № 5. P. 305–332.
14. Fesel B., Sondermann M. 2007. Culture and Creative Industries in Germany // Bonn, 2007. P. 21.

15. Franke R.H., Hofstede G. and Bond M.H. Cultural roots of economic performance: A research note // Strategic Management Journal, 1991. No. 12 (Summer Special Issue). P. 165–173.
16. Garnov A.P., Garnova V.Yu. Innovative Potential of Russia: Problems and Prospects of Realization // RISK: Resources, Information, Supply, Competition. 2016. No. 1. Pp. 92–97 (*in Russian*).
17. Garnov A.P., Kireeva N.S. Logistics Tools: Monograph. 2nd edition, added // M: INFRA-M, 2017. 254 p.
18. Garnov A.P., Kireeva N.S. Financial, Material and Information Flows: Point of Interaction in Logistics // RISK: Resources, Information, Supply, Competition. 2017. No. 2. Pp. 48–51 (*in Russian*).
19. Garnov A.P., Kireeva N.S. Financial, Material and Informational Flows: Interaction Point in Logistics // RISK: Resources, Information, Supply, Competition. 2017. No. 2. Pp. 48–51 (*in Russian*).
20. Garnov A.P., Kireeva N.S. Logistics Tools. Moscow: Creative Economics, 2009 (*in Russian*).
21. Garnov A., Kireeva N. Strategic Planning and Management as Basis for Business Value Increasing by Multi-link Logistics Chains // Logistics. 2012. No. 1(62). Pp. 20–23 (*in Russian*).
22. Garnov A.P., Kireeva N.C. Strategic Planning and Management as a Basis of Business Value Increase by Multi-link Logistics Chains // Logistics. 2012. № 1 (62). Pp. 20–23.
23. Granato J., Inglehart R. and Leblang D. The effect of cultural alues on Economic Development: Theory, Hypotheses, and Some Empirical Tests // American Journal of Political Science. 1996. Vol. 40. No. 3. p. 625.
24. Harrison L. E. Who prospers? How cultural values shape economic and political success. N.Y.: HarperCollins, Basic Books.1992. 288 p.
25. Held D. Introduction to Critical Theory Horkheimer to Habermas / T.W. Adorno. How to look at televise Dion, in the Culture industry. University of California Press. 1980. P. 94–96.
26. Hesmondalgh D. Kultural Industries. 2014. (Russ. ed. A. Mikhalyova), Moscow: HSE (*in Russian*).
27. Howkins, John The creative economy 978-0-140287-94-3.
28. Innovation Resources: Organizational, Financial, Administrative: Studies. no. // Edited by Prof. M. UNITY-DANA, 2003.
29. Katasonov V.Yu. On China Digital Economy // VseSovetnik, online magazine. http://www.vsesovetnik.ru/archives/22055 (*in Russian*).
30. Kireeva N.S. Innovative mechanism of logistics management tools // logistics. 2013. № 1. P. 38–40.

31. Klaus Schwab. Fourth industrial revolution / World Economic Forum®. 2016. Access mode: https://docviewer.yandex.ru/view/40542051.
32. Kupriyanovskii V.Yu. et al. Information Technologies in the System of Universities, Science and Innovation in Digital Economy on UK Example / / International Journal of Open Information Technologies. 2016. V. 4. No. 4. Pp. 30−39.
33. Luttmer E. and Singhal M. Culture, context and the taste for Redistribution // American Economic Journal: Economic Policy. 2011. №3. Pp. 157−177.
34. Malshina N.A. "Culture", "consciousness", "creativity" and "creativity": a comparative approach // Intelligence. Innovations. Investment. 2010. No. 7. Pp. 51−54.
35. Malshina N.A. 2012. Theoretical Bases of Efficiency Increase of Functioning of Logistics Systems Flow Processes of Services Sector on the Basis of Traditional Concepts — Financial Flows // Proceedings of the Saratov University. Ser. Economy. Management. Right. 2012. Vol. 12., Vol.1. Pp. 72−76 (*in Russian*).
36. Malshina N.A. Methodology of Flow Processes Interaction in Logistic Chains of Socio-cultural Service Sysytem // Izvestiya Saratov University. New series. Series: Economics. Management. Right. 2013. T. 13. No. 1−1. Pp. 38−42 (*in Russian*).
37. Malshina N.A. Model of Management Improvement of Flow Processes in Integrated Services Complexes // Saratov University News. New series. Series "Economics. Management. Right" 2014. No. 1. Pp. 163−167 (*in Russian*).
38. Malshina N.A. Organizational and Economic Mechanism of Logistics of Social and Cultural Service Providing Innovative Development of the Volga Region. //Innovative Bulletin of Regions. No. 1. 2013. Pp. 5−11.
39. Malshina N.A., Bryntsev A.N. 2017. Support of Cultural Services through the Integrated Service Centers: Prospects for Development. Journal of Advanced Research in Law and Economics. Fall 2017. Volume VIII. Issue 6(28). Pp. 1827−1839.
40. Materials for the Parliamentary Hearings on February 20, 2018 on "Formation of Legal Conditions for Financing and Development of Digital Economy" // State Duma Committee on Financial Market / URL: http://komitet2-12.km.duma.gov.ru/Novosti-Komiteta/item/15619340 (*in Russian*).

41. Materials on Parliamentary Hearings on February 20, 2018 on "Formation of Legal Conditions for Financing and Development of Digital Economy" // State Duma Committee of Financial Market [electronic resource] – access mode. URL: http://komitet2-12.km.duma. gov.ru/Novosti-Komiteta/item/15619340 (*in Russian*).

42. Melnikov O.N., Larionov V.G., Gankin N.A. Areas of responsibility for the conceptual development of the "creative economy" and "creative industries" // Creative economy. 2015. Vol. 9. No. 3. Pp. 265–278.

43. National accounts 2018 // Federal State Statistics Service-URL: http://www.gks.ru/wps/wcm/connect/rosstat_main/rosstat/ru/statistics/accounts/# (accessed 12.05.2019) (*in Russian*)

44. Newbigin George. Journal of creative economy. Mapping. Moscow: "Creative economy", 2011. P. 80

45. Novikov D.T. 2012. Formation of Logistic Support in the Promotion of Scientific and Technical Developments / RISK. 2012. № 4. Pp. 27 (*in Russian*).

46. Office for National Statistics. URL: https://www.gov.uk (accessed 12.05.2019) (*in Russian*).

47. Orlova T.S. Creativity of economic consciousness of the individual. Tyumen, 2006. 35 p.

48. Plotnikov A.N., Pchelintseva I.N. Management of Social Investment of Microeconomic Systems: Monograph // Saratov. 2009. 173 p.

49. Pontryagin L.S. 1974. Ordinary Differential Equations. 1974. M., Nauka (*in Russian*).

50. Protsenko I.O. Innovative Logistics – Prospects and Realities // Journal of Russian Entrepreneurship. 2005. No. 12 (72). Pp. 89–94. URL: http://www.creativeconomy.ru/articles/7294/ (accessed 12.05.2019) (*in Russian*).

51. Pryor F.L. Cultural riles: a note on economic systems and values // Journal of Economic systems. 2008.Values 36 (3). Pp. 510–515.

52. Rubinstein A.A. Methodology for tracking innovation processes in the regions of the Russian Federation and applied methods for evaluating their innovative activity // Prospects for innovative development of Russian regions. Moscow: IE RAS. 2012. Pp. 265–282. URL: https://inecon.org/docs/Lenchuk_book_2012.pdf.

53. Rubinstein M.F., Firstenberg A.R. Intellectual organization. Bring the future to the present and turn creative ideas into business solutions: TRANS. from English: INFRA-M, 2003. 192 p.

54. Ruda T.V. journal of Creative economy in the system of post-industrial society // Journal of creative economy. 2008. № 8 (20). Pp. 3–11.
55. Science, innovation and Informational Society // Federal State Statistics Service. URL: http://www.gks.ru/wps/wcm/connect/rosstat_main/rosstat/ru/statistics/science_and_innovations/science/# (*in Russian*).
56. Seabrook John. The culture of marketing. Marketing of culture. Moscow: Ad Marginem Press, 2012. 240 p.
57. Sergeev V.I. Management in Business Logistics // M.: INF. ed. House "FILIN", 1997.
58. Socio-economic situation in Russia — 2017 / Federal State Statistics Service-URL: http://www.gks.ru/bgd/regl/b17_01/Main.htm (application date 12. 06.2017) (*in Russian*).
59. State Duma of the Federal Assembly of the Russian Federation // Culture Committee [electronic resource] – access mode. URL: http://komitet2–3.km.duma.gov.EN/upload/site16/Opredelenov.pdf (*in Russian*).
60. Stepanov Yu.S. Language and method. To the modern philosophy of language. Moscow: "Languages of Russian culture". 1998. 787 p.
61. Tabellini G. Culture and Institutions: Economic Development in the Regions of Europe // Journal of the European Economic Association. 2010. No. 8(4). Pp. 677–716.
62. The Order of the Ministry of Culture of the Russian Federation of June 28, 2013 N 920 "About Approval of Methodical Recommendations on Development by Public Authorities of Russian Federation Subjects and by Local Governments of Indicators for Efficiency Activity of Subordinated Culture Institutions, their Heads and Workers by Organization Types and Workers Major Categories". URL: http://www.garant.ru/products/ipo/prime/doc/70327762/#ixzz4nejrFzSc (application date 12.06.2017) (*in Russian*).
63. Throsby D. Economics and Culture // M. Ed. House. Higher School of Economics. 2013. P. 159 (*in Russian*).
64. Zelentsova E.V., Melvil E. Development of creative industries in Russia: problems and prospects // Kulturologicheskiy Zhurnal. 2011. No 4(6). URL: http://www.cr-journal.ru/rus/journals/92.html&j_id=8.